THE BIBLICAL CONCEPT OF MAN

M. M. NINAN

THE BIBLICAL CONCEPT OF MAN

Original Version Juba, Sudan 1987
Revised Versions San Jose, CA 2003, 2010,2013
Normal, IL 2018

ISBN 978-0-359-08497-5
Published by
5708 Rudy Dr., San Jose, CA 95124
http://www.mmninan.com

THE BIBLICAL CONCEPT OF MAN

PROF.M.M.NINAN

THE BIBLICAL CONCEPT OF MAN

PROF.M.M.NINAN

PREFACE

This study on "what is man" was initially done when I was in the Sudan when we started a revival and just started a theological college, in Juba which is now South Sudan's Capital.

Man was created in the image of God. Hence we are looking at what God is and how this characteristic of God is reflected in man. Specifically two characteristics stood up.
God is a Trinity
God is both male and female

Man is the Temple of God and we are given the model of the temple.

Just as God exists in all dimensions, man exists in all dimensions,

It is these that I have tried to present.

Prof.M.M.Ninan

Normal, IL
2018

CHAPTER ONE
IN THE IMAGE OF GOD HE CREATED THEM
A GRAPHIC MODEL

I . MAN AS TRINITY

Man is a complex being. Bible teaches that man is a Trinity consisting of spirit, soul and body. Thus

1 Thess:5:23 says, "May the God of peace himself sanctify you wholly, and may your spirit, soul and body be kept sound and blameless."

Very often the spirit and the soul are confused because of their close affinity and characteristics.

However Hebrews 4:12 says, *"for the word of God is living and active, sharper than any two edged sword piercing to the division of soul and spirit; of joints and marrow; discerning the thoughts and intentions of the heart."*

Thus soul and spirit are distinct entities as the joint and marrow are or thought and the intentions of the heart are. Let us have a look at the three parts of Man as defined by the Holy Scriptures.

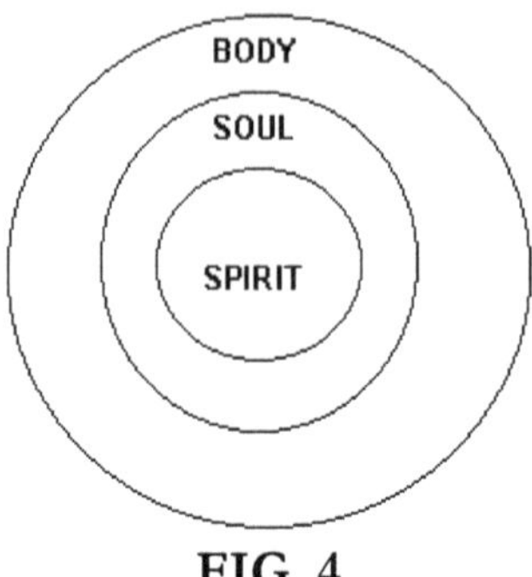

FIG. 4

MODEL OF MAN

BODY

BODY offers no confusion and exists in the three dimensional material world as well as in time. Though we refer to body as one unit it itself is a complex system. Medical science describes the complexity of the body function. Essentially we can divide it into three parts. **Flesh, bones and blood** - each with its own complex systems. The Body has the capacity for **life-function** which also includes **behavioral capabilities**. Both these together produce the life. The Body of man separates him as a distinct entity from the material world. It provides five senses thorough which man get all his information about the external world. These are really not information as such but are simply sensations which are logically analyzed by the brain – mind and then becomes meaningful information. There are five windows of man to the outside world. These are specialized animal function or mechanism such as sight, hearing, smell, taste, and touch which basically involve a stimulus and a sense organ. These are the inputs and one-way valves. Tertullian, (150-220 A.D) explained that the body was the area of "world-consciousness," the soul was the area of "personal-consciousness," and the spirit was the area of "God-consciousness."

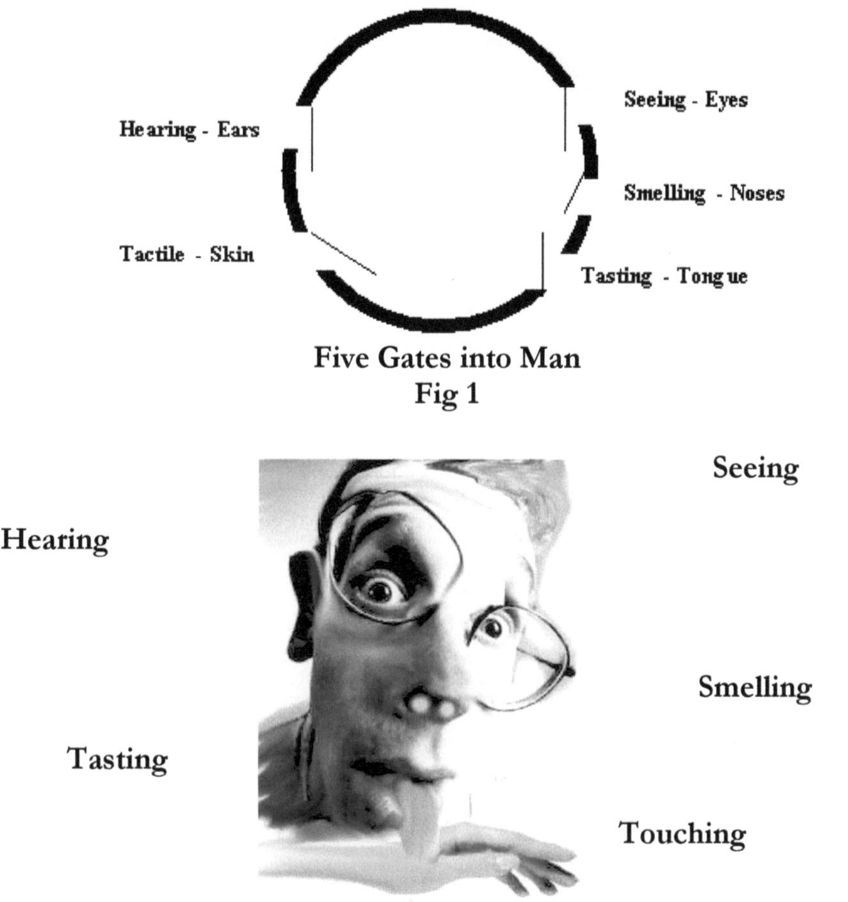

Five Gates into Man
Fig 1

The other parts of the body helps in the input and acts as the output. There are five excretion outlets also. These are: faeces, urine, sperms, sputum, and perspiration.

But there is one outlet which is coming not from the body section but from far within human soul. This is the tongue.

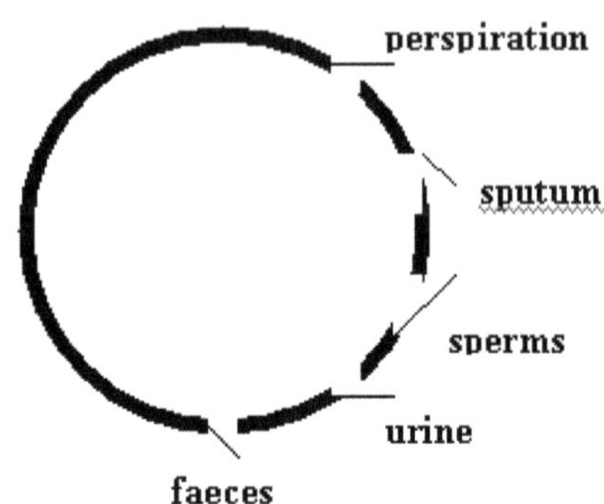

Five Gates out of Man

Fig 2

Mat 15:18 But the things which proceed out of the mouth come forth out of the heart; and they defile the man.

Luk 6:45 The good man out of the good treasure of his heart bringeth forth that which is good; and the evil man out of the evil treasure bringeth forth that which is evil: for out of the abundance of the heart his mouth speaketh.

Jam 3:6 And the tongue is a fire: the world of iniquity among our members is the tongue, which defileth the whole body, and setteth on fire the wheel of nature, and is set on fire by hell.

SOUL

SOUL is associated with the personality of man, his intellect, mind, wisdom, emotions etc. Soul is the field of ideas where experiences are analyzed, stored and interpreted on the basis of previous experiences. Without it events becomes meaningless. Relationships are perceived by the soul. Laws of nature (material and spiritual) are derived in the soul.

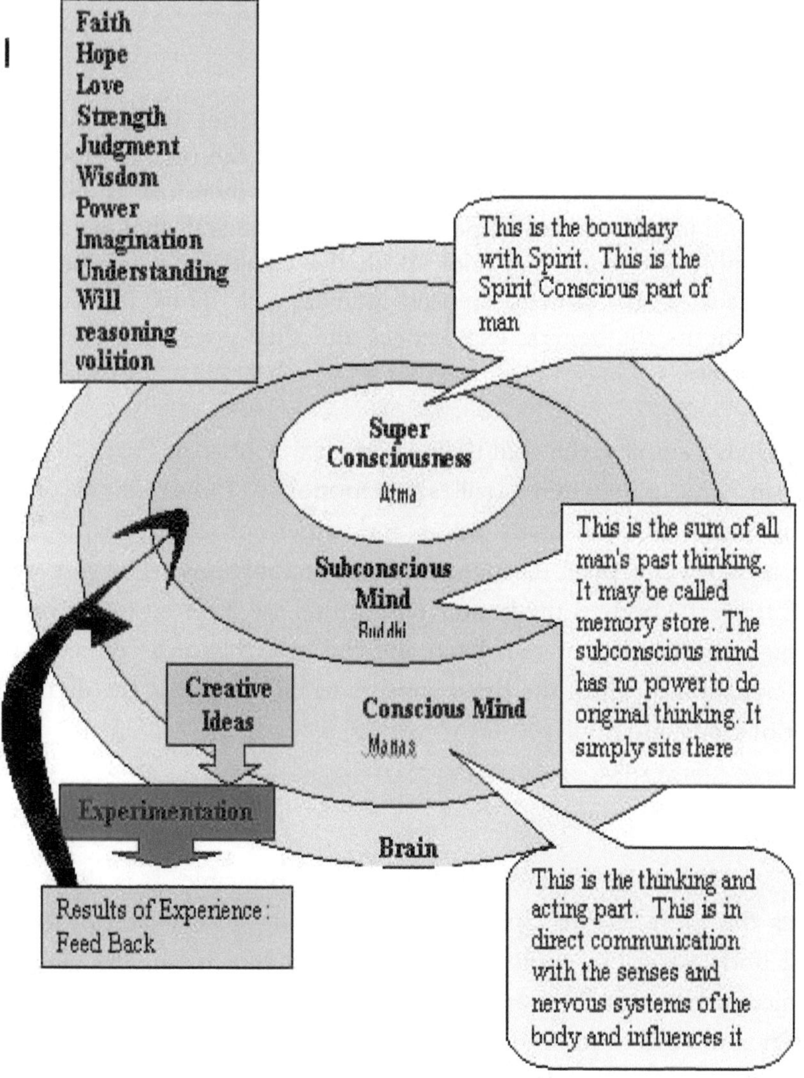

Fig 3

THE SOUL

The observed facts of physical world are simply matter and its motion. The laws of the physical world are perceived out of the mental modeling into velocity, acceleration, force , fields, etc. Soul therefore is the real person as we think of a person's personality. It is the soul that sin and is held responsible for man's behavior. Both the Chaldean word 'nephes' and the Greek word 'psucho' means animal soul. Thus the soul is generated, inherits the generic experiences and then goes on to grow as the person grows.

Just as body is complex, the soul is also complex. Christian Psychologists divide it in three parts: mind ,will and emotions. Others divide it as conscious mind, Subconscious mind and super-conscious mind. The following chart will explain these parts and their functions. The gate way into soul from the body is the brain. The stimuli are directed to the brain where they are decoded or translated and the information is directed to the conscious mind. Thus, the brain appears to be the gate – the dividing assunder of Body and Soul

SPIRIT

SPIRIT is very similar to the soul. It is the life principle. It is the spirit that gives the body its life. Spirit is the life giving go-between between soul and body. It is the spirit that act as a cohesive force, the glue or communicator between the other two dimensions. Without the life giving spirit body and soul cannot coexist. When the spirit leaves the body (i.e. life goes out) the soul separates from the body.

If however the spirit , the soul and the body existed in entirely different dimensions, they could not have interacted as it really does. It should therefore be assumed that they share at least some dimensions with each other. Just as any two perpendicular lines share one common point, or two perpendicular planes share one common line, the three fields of spirit, soul and body must be sharing some points together, either together or pair wise. As the body (which is material - corporal) exists in space-time, soul and spirit must be having their own dimensions of existence. Time is one dimension is common to all the three - or at least by soul and body. But in order to explain the power of the spirit over the body, mind over matter, some other contacts must be present. Except for the sweeping statement,

"the world was created by the Word of God, so that which is seen was made out of things that do not appear." (Heb. 11:3), we do not have any analysis in depth over these matters in the Bible.

A crude model of man, therefore, can be constructed as in fig.4 in page 2. Each reality exists in several dimensions of their own and shares one or more dimensions with each other. Intense interactions takes place between these three fields thus constituting man. We can consider these as sheaths in the traditional Vedic approach of Kosa. I am encouraged and justifies by a similar interpretation given by our Early Father Justin Martyr, the second century father of Christian Apologetics. In his essay on "Resurrection" he uses the model. "The body is the house of the soul, and the soul the house of the spirit." (ca A.D 155) So for the sake of modeling we will use it. We could of course interchange the positions of the spirit and soul to indicate the dependence of body and soul on spirit and that they gets separated if the spirit leave the body. However the analysis that follow will not be affected by this change in the model.

II. GOD AS TRINITY

When God decided to create man God said, "Let us make man in our image after our likeness." "So God created man in his own image, in the image of God, he created him; male and female he created them." Gen. !:26-28 Thus man should in all respects reflect the Trinitarian God, apart from the male and female aspect. The authoritative exposition of Trinity is given by Jesus in Matthew 28:19 as: "in the name of the Father, and of the Son and of the Holy Spirit."

The picture of FATHER is one of a person who does not have a form (Deut. 4:15) Yet he asserts himself as the great "I AM THAT I AM" - the YAHVEH- the Soul of God, the personality of God. (Ex. 3:14). It is the Father who directs the actions and controls as the great supreme person in the Godhead. So the father send the Son into the world. (Jn. 12:19) The Father did sent the Holy Spirit into the world. (Jn. 15:26)

SON is the Word of God out of which all things were created. "He is the image of the invisible God, the first born of all creations; for in him all things were created, in heaven and on earth, visible and invisible, whether thrones or dominions or principalities or authorities - all things were created through him and for him. He is created before all things, and in him all things hold together." Col. 1:15-17 "In him we live and move and have our being." (Act. 17:28) "By faith we understand that the world was created by the Word of God, so that what is seen was made out of things that does not appear." Heb.11 :3 The implication is that Jesus is the pre-matter - the body aspect of God. So as in creation the Word became the matter, the later 'the Word became flesh." Thus the recreation of the world and the redemption of bodies from decay and death, Jesus has the creative role. He provides the resurrected body, but sanctification and acceptance of man's soul will have to proceed from the Father himself. (Heb. 10:10)

The HOLY SPIRIT is the spirit aspect of God. The spirit is the life giving force - the creative force which acting on matter gives birth to life. Thus in Gen. 1:2 "the spirit of God moved upon the face of the earth" in the creation to bring forth life. "Body apart from spirit is dead." (Ja.. 2:26).

"being put to death in flesh, but alive in spirit" (1 Pe. 3:18) "the written word kills, but the spirit gives life to your mortal bodies also through his spirit

which dwells in you." (Rom. 8:11). The Holy Spirit which is coeternal and coequal with Father and Son is the cause of the awareness of the Trinity as unity.

This model of God will be as in Fig. 5.

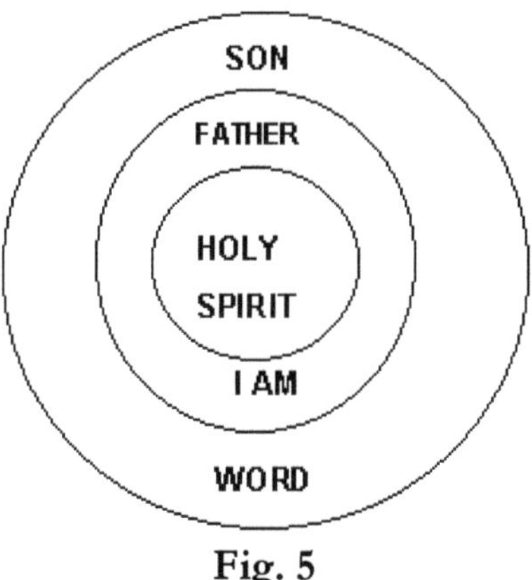

Fig. 5
MODEL OF GOD

Thus man is the image of God as a Trinity, but not in identity as the New Age group, the Hindu Advaitas teach. As the word is different from gross matter, so is the Father Consciousness Self *(The Paramatman)* different from man's consciousness *(Jeevatman)*. However as the Word became matter, God to man relation and difference is one of generation difference, whatever that may mean. This is reflected in the Genealogy of Jesus where Luke states that Adam was the son of God. (Luke 3:38)

God exists in multiple dimensions. Dimensions of Word, Spirit and the Soul. In each dimension his personality is distinct but it is the same God in fullness. This teaching is in essence the teaching of Trinity. Three persons in one God. The three aspects are not aspects of a person seen differently by different people at different occasions as the Monarchists would suggest. Nor are they distinct and separate in the sense of disjointed one emanating from the other or created by the other as the Arians suggest. We will not go into the teaching of Trinity. However this is mentioned here, just to avoid the tendency towards these age old heresies. This study is the study on Man.]

III. THE CREATION OF MAN

Gen. 2:7 describes the act of creation of man thus:, "Then the Lord God formed man of dust from the ground, and breathed into his nostrils the breath of life; and man became a living soul." The body of man is created out of matter the essence of which is Jesus., in whose image it is created and by the Word of God (i.e. Jesus - the Logos) Then God gives the spirit, the breath of life, the essence of which is the Spirit of God. And man became a living soul. God did not create the soul - it came into existence as a result of the interaction of the spirit on matter..

We can see here why man is the likeness of God. The soul belongs to man alone in that he has the right to be what he wants to be. Why God created man like that is a different problem. That is the sovereign will of God. Who are we to question? It remains that man was created with a free will which God respects. The soul is thus a qualitatively new entity evolved out of the interaction of matter and spirit and has an existence by itself. Once generated it grows, gathering more and more experiences. The mind of man stores up all the experiences and its analysis by the intellect for future reference. It is like an immense computer. Human brain contains some ten to the power ten nerve cells which can act in ten to the power eight hundred ways. Compare this with the total number of atoms in the universe which is estimated as ten to the power one hundred only. Thus each human mind is capable of storing the entire data for recreating the entire universe. But soul is not the brain. Brain is only material - a part of the human body. It is the hardware. The soul never decay or die (2 Cor. 5:1), but is "renewed every day". (2 Cor. 4:16). It is renewed in that it revises its entire material on the basis of experience constantly. It updates itself instantly in time. When a man dies, his soul is separated and maintains its identity. The independent existence of the soul outside the body is corroborated in various places in the Bible. In 1 Ki. 17: 17-24 Elijah recalls the soul of the widow's child, and ' the soul of the child returned unto him'. In all the raising of the dead , Jesus recalled the soul that these people came back with the same personality, except probably of updating due to their death experience. It was not giving back life to a dead body that was once the person. It was the return of the person himself. Even in the resurrection of our Lord we see the same . The resurrected Jesus was the same Jesus that the disciples knew. But he was more because of the resurrection. What happens to the soul on death? At death soul goes to a bounded space in the soul dimension. This place is variously called. Two different spaces could be identified. One is called the Sheol (which means the Unseen State) (Ps. 86:13; 16:10; Jon 2:2) and Hades (means the unseen world) (LK 16:23; Act. 2:27,31; Rev. 20:13) or Pits of the Nether Gloom (2 Pe 2:4; Job 33:18-30). It symbolizes a state of existence not in our material space and is gloomy and undesirable. The second place is Paradise which symbolizes a garden ground (Lk. 23:43) - a place of joy where Jesus' presence is given to those whom he loves. It was also called Abraham's Bosom (as in the story of the rich man and Lazarus, which Jesus told.). In both these places the souls remain a separate and distinct existence and they cognates mutually. In this sense death is a reincarnation of man into a different dimension with their total personality.

The spirit of man, returns to God who gave it. (Ec. 12:7). Therefore, at the cross Jesus committed his spirit to God. (Lk 23:46) The spirit is also the seat of wisdom. While the soul is the total compendium of all experiences and intermediate results of analysis and interpretations in the conscious and unconscious mind, the spirit exhibits the final conclusion derived not only from the external experiences but also from the spirit world experience and inferences. Thus the spirit can be broken (Pro. 15:13; 17:22) vexed (Ec. 2:11), haughty (Pro. 16:18), humble (Pro.16:19), wounded (Pro. 18:4), wise, understanding, judging, counseling and mighty (Is. 4:4; 11:2) Heart is considered as the seat of the spirit (Pro. 15:13) Tongue is related to the heart as its display. Thus, "Out of the abundance of the heart, the mouth speaks." (Mat. 12:34-35) Speech often discloses what the state of the heart is. This state is in turn decided by what is fed and stored into the mind from the inception. The child starts with a memory module of genetic heredity and builds on it. Then he has the freedom to change, retain, mend, mould or otherwise grow this soul and spirit states according to his will. Circumstances play a vital role in this growth. Social structure, economic circumstances, educational opportunities, friends and relatives, the personalities of the parents etc. all play a vital role in this growth. However, along with these external factors there is another space from which the spirit gathers its experience and wisdom - i.e. the spirit world.

The relationship between the spirit of man and the spirit of God is a complex problem. Most Christian thinkers consider it as basic that they are two different entities - Paramatma and Jeevatman dual.. Christian philosophy is Dvaitic. In the figure 2, we have depicted it as sealed or housed (in Justin's terminology) inner most sheath of man (Job. 27:3; 32:8). These sheaths in the Hindu thought are divided into seven Kosas and the atma is identified as the combination of spirit and soul. If we assume that the spirit of man is the same as the spirit of God as in the sense of water of the sea can be separated off into pools and lake, we have the advaitic approach justified. Here man does not become God as Hindu philosophy argues. The presence of the spirit of God in man does not make him God. It only gives man the experience of God through the spirit. This spirit simply returns to God while the soul of man remains an entity apart from his body. "It is the Spirit himself that bears witness with our spirit that we are children of God." (Rom. 8:16)

It is interesting here to compare the creative process between man and the rest of the living beings on earth. The living creatures actually were created by an evolutionary process. Notice the process as described in Genesis. "God said, "let the earth put forth vegetation, plants yielding seed and fruit trees bearing fruit in which is their seed, each according to its kind, upon the earth'" And it was so." (Gen. 1:11) Similarly in the creation of water creatures it says, "And God said, " Let the water bring forth swarms of living creatures, and let birds fly above the earth across the firmament of the heavens" So God created..." (Gen. 1:20-21) Then the bible goes on to describe the creatures of the land using similar words, "And God said, "Let the earth bring forth living creatures according to their kind....." (Gen. 1:24-25) The General formula seems to be: And God said, "Let ...... bring forth ......after its kind....." Therefore, we have the creative word, which brings forth life, evolves life from the created world. We see no direct intervention of the spirit of God except that of the brooding over (moving over the face of the waters) the matter . Man was also created out of the existing material. In this case, we have the following description. ""Then the Lord God formed man of dust from the ground, and breathed into his nostrils the breath of life; and man became a living soul." Here is the direct intervention of breathing which makes man distinct from animals. There is that special direct touch of God in the creation of man. Otherwise, man and the rest of the creatures on the earth are identical. In fact, God expected man to find a helper from among the creatures. "But for the man there was not found a helper fit for him." because he was distinctly different.

Ecclesiastes declares the great similarity thus: "For the fate of the sons of men and the fate of the beasts is the same; one dies, so dies the other. They all have the same breath, and man has no advantage over the beasts; for all is vanity. All go to one place; all are from dust, and all turn to dust again. Who knows whether the spirit of man goes upward and the spirit of the beast goes down to the earth? " (Ecc. 3: 19-21) Ecclesiastes therefore perceives that the difference between man and beast is to be found in the spirit that is in man and beast. It is somehow different but still similar. One thing is sure, " ...man goes to his eternal home.....the dust returns to earth as it was, and the spirit returns to God who gave it." (Ecc.11:5-7) In the creation story, we saw that the spirits of creatures were derived from the spirit that created and conglomerated the cosmos. We do not have any correct idea about the spirit of animals. It is certainly different from that of man. Whereas the spirit of man was given directly by God into his nostrils the spirit of beasts were derived from the cosmic creative spirit inherent in the created world..

IV. JESUS: SON OF MAN AND SON OF GOD

As in the Genesis creation of the man, Jesus was also taken out of the flesh of man, which was originally taken out of the dust, through Mary, in whom the enveloping (overshadowing) of the Holy Spirit created a living soul. The differences here are first the material was not plain dust, but flesh; second that the spirit within Jesus was Holy Spirit,

he Paramatma and not the spirit of man, Jeevatma. The resultant soul generated, developed in this world and is therefore a perfect man. Thus, the model of Jesus in our modeling system will look as in figure 6

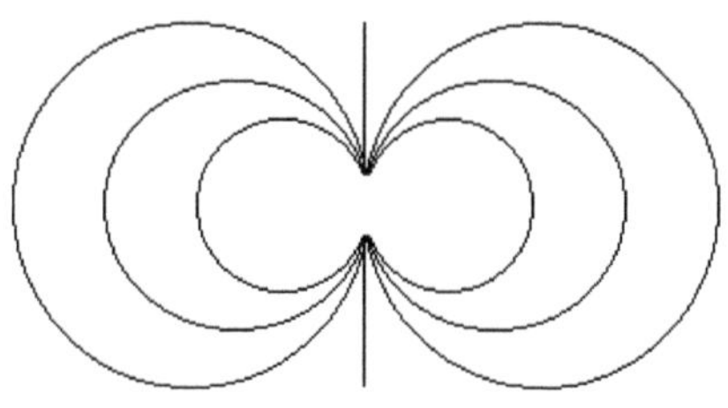

DIVINE PLANE HUMAN PLANE

FIG. 6
JESUS: PERFECT GOD & PERFECT MAN

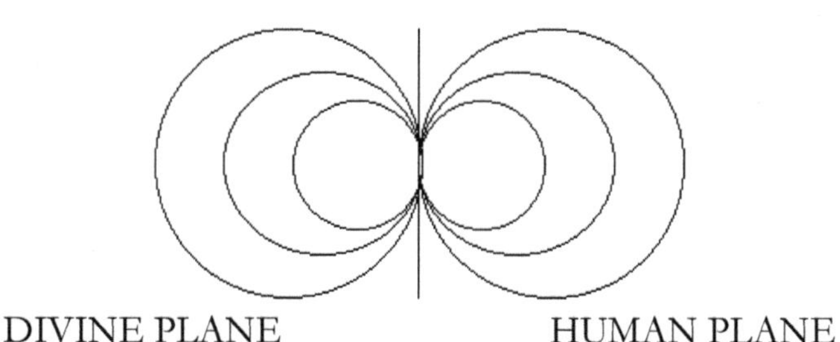

FIG. 7
PERFECT MAN

MAN AS A THREE DIMENSIONAL BEING

We have seen that man can be thought of as a being, which came into existence as a result of the coming in together of the Spirit and Matter – the two components used in the creation of man.

The material man – the body – reflects as in a mirror, the spiritual man. Body is made out of matter and the spirit body (astral body as some calls it) is made of spiritual material.

1Co 15:44 … If there is a natural body, there is also a spiritual body.

Joh 3:6 That which is born of the flesh is flesh; and that which is born of the Spirit is spirit.

Joh 6:63 It is the spirit that giveth life; the flesh profiteth nothing:

Rom 8:4 that the ordinance of the law might be fulfilled in us, who walk not after the flesh, but after the Spirit.

Rom 8:5 For they that are after the flesh mind the things of the flesh; but they that are after the Spirit the things of the Spirit.

Rom 8:6 For the mind of the flesh is death; but the mind of the Spirit is life and peace:

Rom 8:7 because the mind of the flesh is enmity against God; for it is not subject to the law of God, neither indeed can it be:

Rom 8:8 and they that are in the flesh cannot please God.

If we live according to the flesh, i.e. when we are not being led by the Spirit of God, we are being led by: sight, sound, smell, touch, and taste.

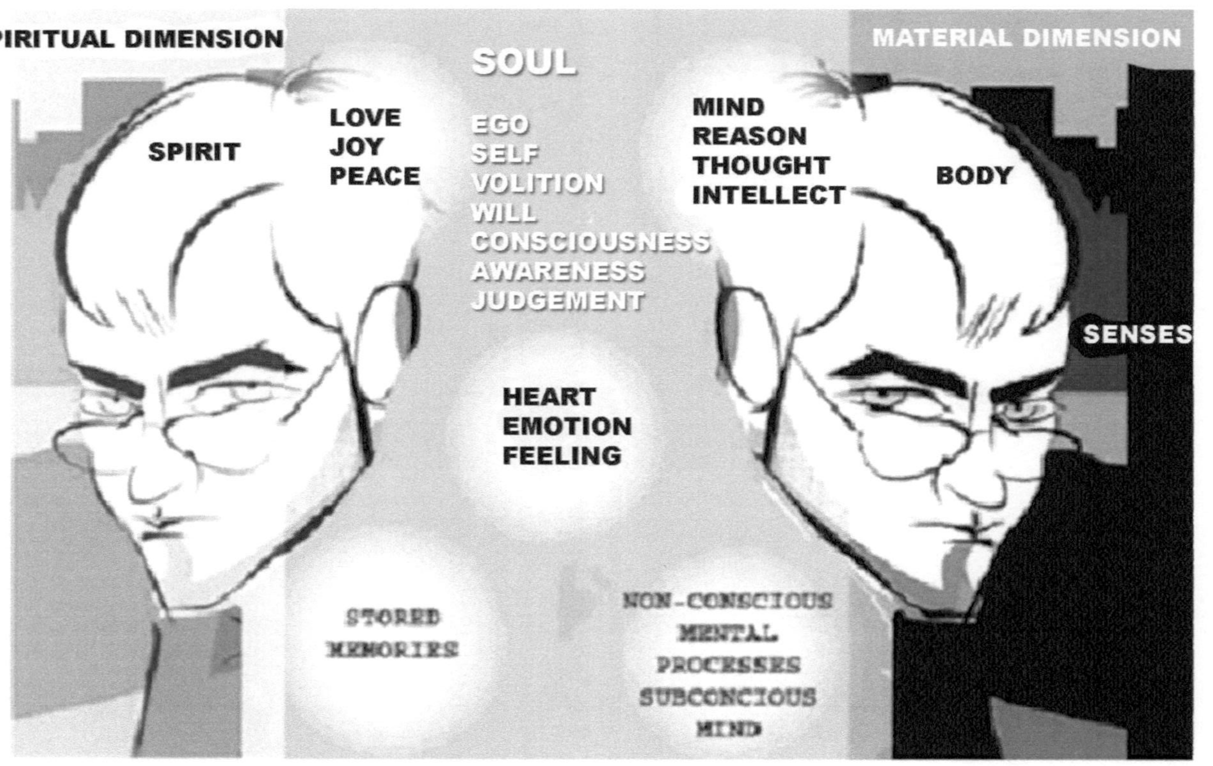

Fig. 8

TWO DIMENSIONS OF MAN

BEYOND THE SPIRIT INTO THE DIVINE

Rom 8:9 But ye are not in the flesh but in the Spirit, if so be that the Spirit of God dwelleth in you. But if any man hath not the Spirit of Christ, he is none of his.

Rom 8:10 And if Christ is in you, the body is dead because of sin; but the spirit is life because of righteousness.

Rom 8:11 But if the Spirit of him that raised up Jesus from the dead dwelleth in you, he that raised up Christ Jesus from the dead shall give life also to your mortal bodies through his Spirit that dwelleth in you.

Rom 8:12 So then, brethren, we are debtors, not to the flesh, to live after the flesh:

Rom 8:13 for if ye live after the flesh, ye must die; but if by the Spirit ye put to death the deeds of the body, ye shall live.

Rom 8:14 For as many as are led by the Spirit of God, these are sons of God.

Rom 8:15 For ye received not the spirit of bondage again unto fear; but ye received the spirit of adoption, whereby we cry, Abba, Father.

Rom 8:16 The Spirit himself beareth witness with our spirit, that we are children of God:

Rom 8:17 and if children, then heirs; heirs of God, and joint-heirs with Christ; if so be that we suffer with him, that we may be also glorified with him.

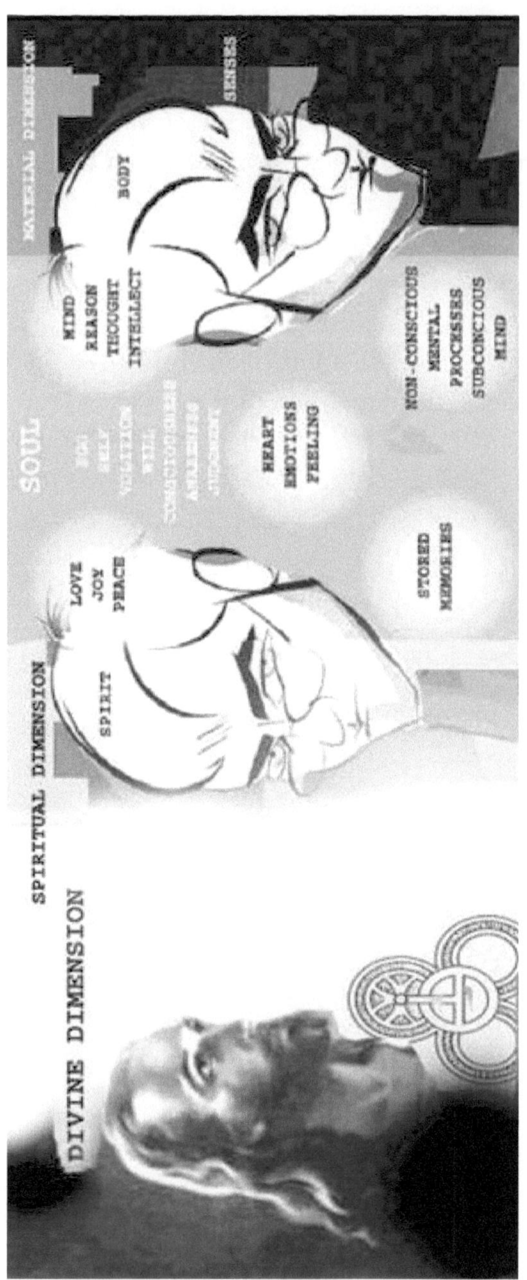

Fig. 9

THEOSIS

When man was created, Adam had the freedom in both spiritual and material dimensions. However as he received the sense stimuli from the spirit world from Satan, God closed the gates from spirit world into the soul in order to protect man. Today no spirit can enter the soul without the expressed permission from the soul. This also meant that even the Holy Spirit cannot enter a human heart except when he willfully accepts the Holy Spirit.

Once the Holy Spirit enters the spirit of man it opens up a totally new dimension of existence – the dimension of the Divine.

2Co 3:18 And we all, with unveiled face, beholding the glory of the Lord, are being changed into his likeness from one degree of glory to another; for this comes from the Lord who is the Spirit.

CHAPTER TWO

YOU ARE THE TEMPLE OF GOD

I. THE TEMPLE

Of man it is said, "You are the temple of God." (2 Cor. 6:16; 1 Cor. 3:16-17; Jn. 2: 19-21. So it is instructive to see how man resembles the temple and what lessons this model given by God gives us.

The temple was built up precisely according to the plan that was given by God in the Sinai Mountain to Moses, while he was with God. (Ex. 25:8-9:30). A detailed description of the temple and all the furniture in it are found in Ex. 25:10 - 30:38 and in Ex. 35:1-39:43. A short summary is given in Ex. 40 and also in Hebrews 9:1-10. We will summarize this in figure 6 in the next page giving the plan and position of the furniture.

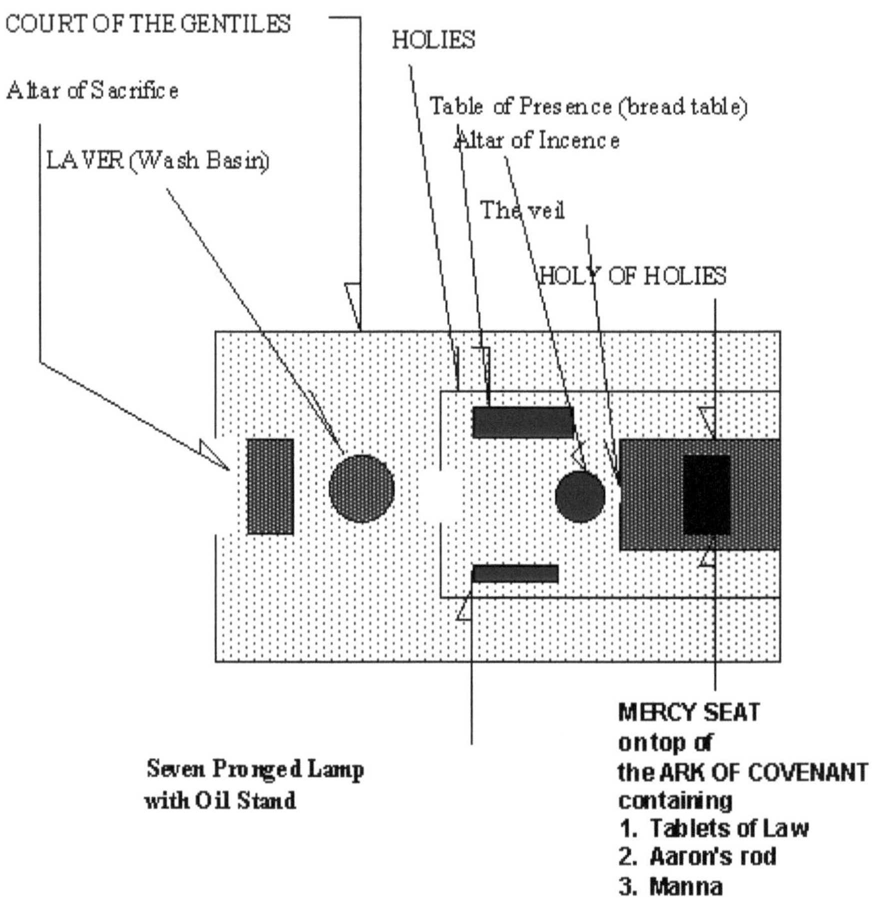

Fig 1

THE TEMPLE
AS GIVEN TO MOSES BY GOD

We can immediately see the correlation with the figures 1 and 2 in the Trinitarian image.

Here is the comparison:

THE BIBLICAL CONCEPT OF MAN

TEMPLE	MAN	GOD
Outer Court or Court of the Gentiles This is the area of communication and contact with external world	Body with it senses	Jesus The Word of God
The Assembly Hall or The Holies This is the area of inner communications of identity and ego	Soul "I AM"	Father "I AM"
The Inner Sanctuary or The Holy of Holies This is the area of life giving force.	Spirit	Holy Spirit
Ark of the covenant and the Mercy Seat. God speaks directly to Man	The divine realm	The Unity of God

The Temple though given to the Jews in the Old Covenant, also represents the organism of Church. In this comparison, the Body of Christ consists of individual believers all over the world and in all time. Their life and witness are outreach of the church, which communicates, with the rest of the gentile world. The soul of the church is the oneness of mind of the saints (the assembly). The Holy Spirit was given to the Church at the time of Pentecost. Thus, the church is an organic person, with its body, mind and the Holy Spirit and forms the bride of Christ. We could then add another column for the church to the above tabulation. Again, in the next section we will see that Hebrews 9 the author indicates that the temple also indicates the growth of the Christian church through history. Invariably by comparison, it also indicates human growth from childhood, youth and fatherhood as the Christian's growth to maturity. This is clearly expanded in the letters of John. See 1 John 7-14.

Then we could add three additional columns of comparison as follows.

THE TEMPLE	**THE CHURCH ORGANISM**	**CHURCH AGE (Historically)**	**MAN'S AGE & BELIEVER'S GROWTH**
Outer Court	Christians as living Witness in Community Missions Humanitarian and Outreach Ministries	Orthodox . Period	childhood Ritualistic
The Assembly.	Fellowship of the saints Believers' gathering for edification, support and growth Common worship	Reformation Period	youth
Holy of Holies	Believers' fellowship with God Worship in Spirit and Truth	?	father
Mercy Seat	Union with Jesus		Beyond Life – the abundant life

II THE OUTER COURT

The outer court is the body of man. Here we come in contact with the rest of the mankind and with the physical world. Through the five senses, we perceive this world and express ourselves through our body. This is the interactive field with the external world.

In God, the outer court, the body is the Word. It is the word that created the physical world. It is the Word that maintained the physical world. God deals with sinful man through Jesus - the Word who became flesh. God cannot communicate with the world except through the Word, incarnate or otherwise, because that is only point of contact and in the same dimension between God and fallen man. After the Ascension of Jesus, Church is that body with Jesus as its head. (Col 1:18) Thus, today God interacts with the rest of the mankind through the Church. It is the members of the Church as members of the body who have the responsibility of giving the Word of God to the rest of the world and to keep the society from decaying. "You are the salt of the earth" . "You are the light of the world." (Mt. 5: 13,14)

The temple is also the place of worship. Thus, it signifies the dynamics of redemption of man as also the human approach to God -as he enters from the outer court to the Holy of Holies for worship. The carnal man is body centered. "Those who live according to the flesh set their minds on the flesh...To set the mind on flesh is death." (Rom. 8:5,6) Before he can even think of approaching God, he needs to be reconciles with Good. There is only one gate to the temple. Jesus said, ""I am the way>" (Jn 14:6), "I am the door>" (Jn. 10:7,9) "And you, who once were estranged and hostile in mind, doing evil deeds, he has now reconciled in his body of flesh by his death, in order to present you holy..." (Col. 1:21,22) "And there is salvation in no one else, for there is no other name given among men by which we must be saved." (Act. 4:12)

In the outer court itself, an eternal forgiveness of sins and cleansing is available to us in Jesus. This is represented by the altar of sacrifice and the brazen laver. Hebrews 10 describes the difference between Israel and the Church. "We have been sanctified through the offering of the body of

Jesus Christ, once and for all." (Heb. 10:10) Through him then let us continually offer up sacrifices of praise to God, that is the fruit of the lips that acknowledge him. (Heb. 13:14-15) There is thus a once and for all act of acceptance of Jesus as your sacrifice in accordance with the law. (Lev. 16:8-12) and a continual offering of praise. It is clear that the Lord's Table is not a sacrifice. If you are already born again, the only sacrifice now needed is the sacrifice of praise. This sacrifice is brought to the Holy of Holies by the Royal High Priests. No other ritual is taught in the bible under the new covenant. If symbols are to be used as a means of communications, use them. All communications must involve symbols, either audible or visible or oleofatic. But do not make it an idol. If it becomes an idol, break it into pieces even it is considered most sacred. 1 Ki. 18:3 tells us a story of the destruction of such a holy relic viz. the brazen serpent that Moses lifted up in the wilderness. We know that it represented Jesus, but it was not Jesus and hence it has to be destroyed. For the unregenerate ritualism is a necessity to constantly remind them of the necessity of cleansing, of their slavery to the gods of this world who cannot save.

Once redeemed by the sacrifice of Jesus, the believer is to cleanse himself daily from the water in the laver - symbol of washing with the Word of God. (Eph. 5:26) "He who has washed (in the blood of Jesus Rev. 7:14; 1 Cor. 6:11) does not need to wash, except his feet, because he is in contact with the world in his daily interaction and walk. He does not require a fresh sacrifice, only washing of the feet is required. "If any one sin, we have an advocate with the father, Jesus Christ, the righteous, and he is the expiation for our sins and cleanses us from all unrighteousness. (1 Jn. 1:9)

In the outer court, the worship is essentially ritualistic simply because we are in the material physical dimension. They certainly shadows the reality of self-sacrifice and the need for cleansing from sin continuously. This is the first step in man's approach to God in worship. written word kills, but it is the spirit that gives life. When understood in terms of the spirit in which the word is written it realizes growth. Word by itself is legalism. Food by itself is flabbiness. The body will eventually succumb to its own weight. This is what happened to the Pharisees at the time of Jesus. Spirit by itself without the Word is fanaticism. It is typified in the Jewish system of temple worship. Most of it is ritual centered. Most, if not all religion, excluding Christianity, fall into this group. Many Christian groups and denominations also fall into this category. They go to church (some churches has compulsory days of attendance) , repeat prayers or chanting, making of the sign of the cross, carrying of the cross, kissing the book, kneeling before images and icons or altar, take home and revere relics and symbols etc. Hebrews 9:6-10 describes this situation, "By this the Holy Spirit indicates that the way to sanctuary is not yet opened as long as the outer tent (the tabernacle) is still standing. (Which is the symbol of the present age) { the Early Church Age}. According to this arrangement...... regulations of the body were imposed until the time of reformation." What is this reformation? Reformation in church history took place at the time of Luther and Calvin. The church continued to be ritual centered until that time at least from 315 A.D. It also implies that we will not be able to realize true worship in spirit until the time of transformation of our bodies. Hebrew author reefers to the temple structure in terms of the ages in the church leads us to think that the temple also indicates not only man's journey to God; but also the how church grows into the likeness of Jesus. It tells us the historical development of the church in becoming the bride of Jesus. The ritualistic church of the Orthodox period is the entry of the church in the outer court. It was only the beginning of the total redemption of mankind.

Chronologically this is man in childhood. This is the time the baby learns about his external world through his five senses. In the growth of the Christian, this is the initial stage when the person comes to know Jesus and his sins are forgiven and he is given a clean slate to start with.. "I am writing to you, little children, because your sins are forgiven, for his sake." "I write to you, children, because you know the Father." (1 Jn. 2:12-13)

III THE HOLIES

The inner court is the court of the redeemed - the meeting hall for the congregation of the chosen ones. No non-Jew is allowed inside this Assembly Hall. No sinner even from among the Jew is permitted inside until they have been atoned by sacrifice. This is the soul of the people of God. Here members of the community commune with each other, share their burdens, help each other, worship together, learn together, discuss all matters concerning the society. This indeed is the true character of the redeemed community of God. This is the soul of the church. Here the redeemed shall gather together to worship and to grow as an organism. "Let us consider how to stir up one another to love and to do good works; not neglecting to meet together, as is the habit of some; but encouraging another..." (Heb. 10: 24,25)

There are three elements of furniture in the Holies that signify the nature and function of this part of the temple. These are the Table of Presence or the Bread Table, the Incense Table and the Six Pronged Lamp with Oil Stand. The Shew Bread Table made of gold carries twelve loaves of bread one for each tribe of Israel made of unleavened flour dough. This is renewed every Sabbath and the bread are eaten by the Priests and the Levite. The bread is interleaved and anointed with incense. Bread represents the need of constant feeding on the Word of God for the growth and strength of the Church. One function of the Church is to read and ingest the written word of God and to realize in their personal life the

living Word of God - Jesus. "I am the living bread, he who comes to me shall not hunger, and he who believes in me shall never thirst." (Jn. 6:35) "I am the living bread which came down from heaven.." (Jn.6:48) But the written word must be mixed with incense, the spirit so that it becomes life-giving word. The Fanaticism will only cause its own destruction, as it degenerates into myths and fancies. Word with Spirit is growth and Strength. In every believer, Christ likeness is produced only by continual feeding of the Word in Spirit. This is represented in the church in the breaking of bread and the ministry of the Word. In the case of natural man, it represents the youth, caused by the feeding materials of food, mind-feeding materials of books that we read, the friends that we have, the movies that we see, the people with whom we work with etc. We have a choice to accept or reject in these. In some cases, we ingest it, and in other cases, we reject it. There is a constant fight and struggle in this area. It is this exercise of muscles that builds us into strong men. In the same way, it is the exercise of our faith that builds us into strong believers. Thus, John addresses the young men thus: "I am writing to you young men, because you have overcome the evil one.... I write to you young men because you are strong, and the word of God abides in you, and you have overcome the evil one>" (1 Jn. 2:13-14)

The second furniture is the Seven Pronged Lamp with Oil Stand. Lamp is meant to shine forth - to illuminate and to show clearly. The word in Greek actually mean : to manifest or to make known. The original Greek word for lamp stand is a feminine form of the yoke of a plow or the beam. It represents an exercise, or work through the power supplied to it. Mere feeding will not produce healthy tissues. It has to be exercised. This is enabled by the potential energy obtained from the oil. Oil therefore represents the Holy Spirit, which empower the Church and the believer to effectively minister to the community. The gifts of the Holy Spirit are given to every believer and to the church for the edification and growth of the Church. It is the spirit within every man that enable man to perform in their gifts effectively. The gifts blooms in youth.

There are several manifestations of the Holy Spirit. This is represented in the seven-pronged lamp. The sevenfold spirit of God is mentioned in

Rev. 4:15. Some of these are mentioned in Isaiah. These are "the spirit of wisdom, and of understanding, the spirit of counsel and might, the spirit of knowledge and the fear of the Lord, " (Is.11:2) ; "and the spirit of judgment (justice)" (Is. 28:6)

The incense table represents the worship rendered congregational by the church and individually within every believer. This is the meditative aspect of man - the soul's contact point with the spirit world. A man is determined by the God or gods he worship. Many people contend that it does not matter what or in whom you believe as long as the behavior and conduct are right. But your actions are determined by the worldview you hold and this in turn is decided by what you believe in your heart. "Out of the abundance of heart, the mouth speaks." Our speech and actions are nothing but the outcome of our inner soul state. If we think negatively, it will result eventually in destruction, defeat and death. If we think positively, it liberates and creates. This is true of the carnal man as well as of the spiritual man. Hence, through out the Bible, we have an emphasis on

feeding and meditating on the word of God. "This book of the law shall not depart out of your mouth, but you shall meditate on it day and night, that you may be careful to do according to all that is in it; for then you shall make your way prosperous and then you shall have good success." Hence, Paul gives the advice to all men, which is valid both in carnal sphere as well as in spiritual sphere. "Finally brethren, whatever is true, whatever is honorable, whatever is just, whatever is pure whatever is lovely, whatever is gracious, if there be any excellence, if there is anything worthy of praise, think about these things." (Phill. 4:8)

The incense altar represent the prayer and worship. This is a prayer with understanding - a conscious intellectual activity. In Cor. 14:15 Paul clarifies this type of prayer as distinct from praying in the spirit. However,

Heb. 9:4 indicates that the altar of incense actually belongs to the inner sanctuary - the Holy of Holies and is lent to the Holies to the Assembly.

Thus, we may understand that prayer and worship has dimensions beyond the intellect, beyond mind and soul into the sphere of spirit. You may start praying in understanding

and go on into praying in the spirit. As we start worshipping in our mind and intellect, we drift into the sphere of the spirit to worship the Lord in spirit and truth. Thus, the incense altar is placed in front of the veil that separates the Holies from the Holy of Holies. Now Jesus has torn this veil from top to bottom at his sacrifice in the cross, that we may enter into the Holy of Holies. The veil no longer exists for the worshipper. Hence, the confusion of the soul and the spirit is understandable.

In the growth of the Church, this represents the Congregational Era. If the Orthodoxy was based on external ceremonies, the new era opened the Church where the emphasis was on the people as a community. The clergy based church gave way to people based churches. Bible was given to every one and the spirit gave gifts to all believers bringing for evidences of miracles, healing, prophecy, ability to teach, interpret etc. This is the period following the Reformation. In this era the emphasis on intellect. The faith was justified in terms of reason. The characteristics of the Church is the 'oneness of mind and spirit'. Essentials of Christian growth is enunciated in Act. 2:42. "They devoted themselves to (1) the apostles teaching, (2) Fellowship, (3) to the breaking of bread and (4) prayer."

IV .THE HOLY OF HOLIES

A summary description of the inner sanctuary is given in Hebrews 9:3-5. "Behind the second curtain stood a tent called Holy of Holies, having the golden altar of incense and the ark of the covenant covered on all sides with gold, which contained a golden urn holding manna, the Aaron's rod that budded, and the tables of the covenant; above it were the cherubim of glory overshadowing the mercy seat." There was the thick curtain separating the Holy of Holies from the Holies. Into this the High Priest alone went, and that too only once in a year, "and not without taking the blood which he offers for himself and for the errors of the people." (Heb.9:7; Lev. 16:1-19)

Entering into the presence of a most Holy God was an owe inspiring and risky job, because he "will by no means clear the guilty." (Ex. 34:7) Hence special golden bells were sewn into the skirts of the High Priest, 'and its sound shall be heard when he goes into the holy place before the Lord, and when he comes out, lest he die." (Ex. 28:34) Thus, people could know that he is alive. However, as an additional precaution a chain was attached to the leg of the High Priest so that in case he was struck by God, due to iniquity he could be pulled out. Such was the awesome nature of the abode of the inner sanctuary. "There I (God) will meet with you, and above the mercy seat, from between the two Cherubim that are upon the ark of the testimony I will speak with you." (Ex. 25:17-22)

The ark represents the spirit of man, the mercy seat is placed over it where the glory of the God appears and speaks with man. Ark as the seat of the spirit of man resents the hearts of man. In it are (1) the tablets of the law, (2) Aaron's Rod, (3) Manna. When a law is external, man will have to adhere to it by the force of punishment. But once the law is written inside the heart, he will know it and do it without external compulsion, because that is his nature. The law was originally written in the hearts of every man. But they have become hard due to sinfulness. The promise of God had been "I will give them one heart (all the people) and put a new spirit within them; I will take the stony heart out of their flesh and give them a heart of flesh, that they will walk in my ordinances and obey them. They shall be my people and I will be their God." (Ex. 11:19-20) "I will put my law within them, and I will write them upon their hearts., and I will be their God, and they shall be my people, and no longer shall each man teach his neighbor and teach his brother, saying, 'Know the Lord", for they shall all know me, from the least of them to the greatest." (Jer. 31:33-34) By putting the Spirit of God as counselor within the spirit of man from the time of Pentecost this promise is being fulfilled in the believer.

The rod of Aaron is the rod that has done wonders in the wilderness as well as in Egypt. It swallowed up all the serpents of the Egyptian magicians (Ex. 7:10-15) and it did all the wonders over nature during the plagues that were imposed on Pharaoh and the Egyptians. (Ex. 8-14; 16;17:5-9); it gave power of decision and choice (Num. 17:2-9); brought forth water from the rock (Num. 17:2-9) and divided the Red Sea for Israel to pass through. It is the rod of authority and power over all the world, over all principalities and powers of darkness even in the high places and over nature. This power is there in a limited sense within every man, but enlivened and living in every believer and the church of God on earth.

Manna is the total requirement for living. It gave all the nourishment required by the body for the Israelites throughout their forty years of sojourn and wilderness. Hence it is symbolical of the fulfillment of all human requirements in the body, in the society and in the spirit. Thus, manna is described often as the spiritual food. The point here is that the power to transcend moral laws, natural laws and to have power and authority over nature and beings are within the reach of every man, as it was given to Adam. The tablets of law, the rod and the urn of manna are there. In the natural man, this power rests on the understanding of the natural laws and applying it. Science and Arts are employed to achieve power over man and nature. In that respect, it is possible to reach them by inner meditation as Hindu thought strives. By understanding, the laws that exists in the spirit world power can be obtained. However unless we can enter into the Holy of Holies this cannot be done. But once you are in it i.e. if you can enter without being destroyed - you can have these powers. Otherwise, you will have to pay the price, which is destruction and death. Magic and witchcraft rely on these powers at its own price. "But when Christ had offered for all time a single sacrifice for sins, he sat down at the right hand of God, then to wait until his enemies are made a stool for his feet. For by a single sacrifice he has perfected for all time those who were sanctified.... Therefore, brethren, since we have confidence to enter the sanctuary by the blood of Jesus, by the new and living way which he opened for us through the curtain, that is through his flesh, and since we have a great high priest over the house of God, let us draw near with a true heart in full assurance of faith." (Heb. 10:10-22)

Aaron's rod that budded is symbolical of the resurrected Jesus. It is the name of Jesus that has the power over everything - "that at the name of Jesus, every knee shall bow." (Rom. 14:11) The name of Jesus is 'far above all rule and authority and power and dominion, and above every name that is named." and this name and authority is given to the church. (Eph. 1:21-23) Again, Jesus is the manna that came down from heaven, not such as the fathers ate and died; he who eats this manna will live forever. (Jn. 6:58)

Jesus said, "And these signs will accompany those who believe, in my name they will cast out demons. They will speak in new tongues; they will pick up serpents; and if they drink any deadly thing they will recover." (Mk 16:17-18) "In that day .... you ask anything of the Father, he will give it you in my name." (Jn. 16:23) But why not all Christians enjoy these privileges and promises. Because they have not yet got the courage to enter into the holy of holies. The essential onus lie in the church itself. The intellectual church teaches intellectual things. It has been teaching elementary doctrines, emphasizing how sinful man is, how unworthy a dust and a worm he is. It treats Christians as babes and refuses to let them grow into maturity and to the full freedom of man in Christ Jesus. "Therefore let us leave the elementary doctrines of Christ and go on to maturity, not laying again a foundation of repentance from dead works and of faith toward God; with instructions about ablutions, the laying on of hands, and the resurrection of the dead, and eternal judgment. And this we will do if God permits. " (Heb. 6:1-3)

Today churches all over the world irrespective of denominational differences and theological differences are finding new dimensions in the spirit, new ways of worship and new power that rises out of this entry into the Holy of Holies.

In the chronological development of man, this is the fatherhood of man, where he is mature and calm with depth of wisdom and understanding.

In the individual Christian, this stage is the Fatherhood as referred to in John 2:13-14 thus, "I am writing to you fathers because you know him who is from the beginning....." The mature Christian knows the God, the Ancient One. This is the stage we all look forward to.

TEMPLE MAN

Recent research by Tony Badillo suggests that the Solomon's temple might have been built actually in the form a man. Jewish Kabalistic tradition holds that the Temple was built in the image of Adam Kadamon, the ideal man. The floor plan reveals half man while the vertical structures indicates the remainder of man. (see Mishkan (tabernacle): did it have a hidden human form? Tony Badillo)

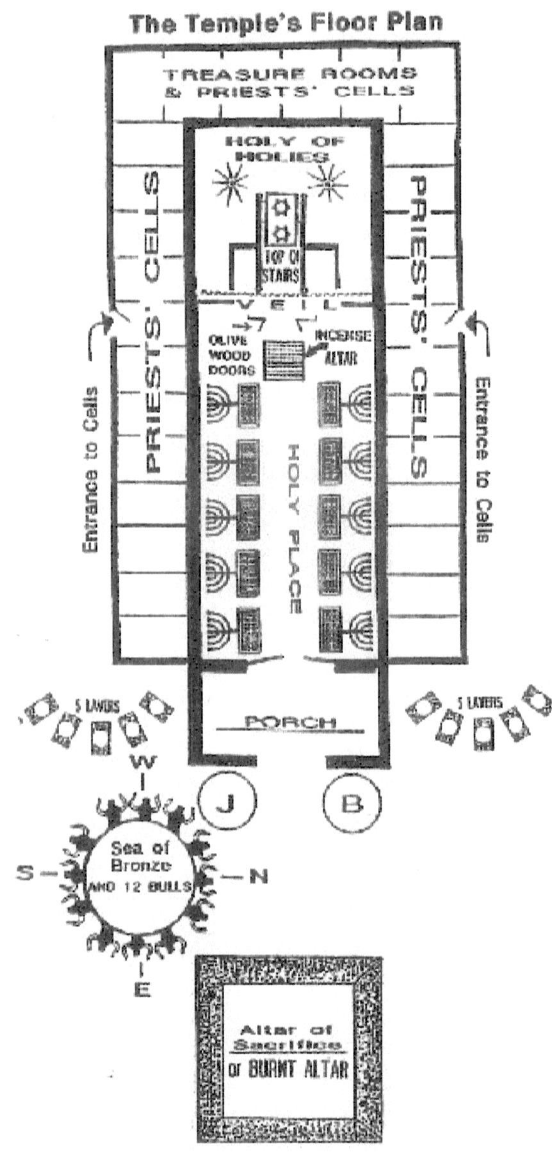
The Temple's Floor Plan
TREASURE ROOMS
& PRIESTS' CELLS
HOLY OF
HOLIES
TOP OF
STAIRS
VEIL
OLIVE
WOOD
DOORS
INCENSE
ALTAR
PRIESTS' CELLS
PRIESTS' CELLS
HOLY PLACE
Entrance to Cells
Entrance to Cells
5 LAVERS
5 LAVERS
PORCH
W
J
B
Sea of
Bronze
AND 12 BULLS
S
N
E
Altar of
Sacrifice
or BURNT ALTAR

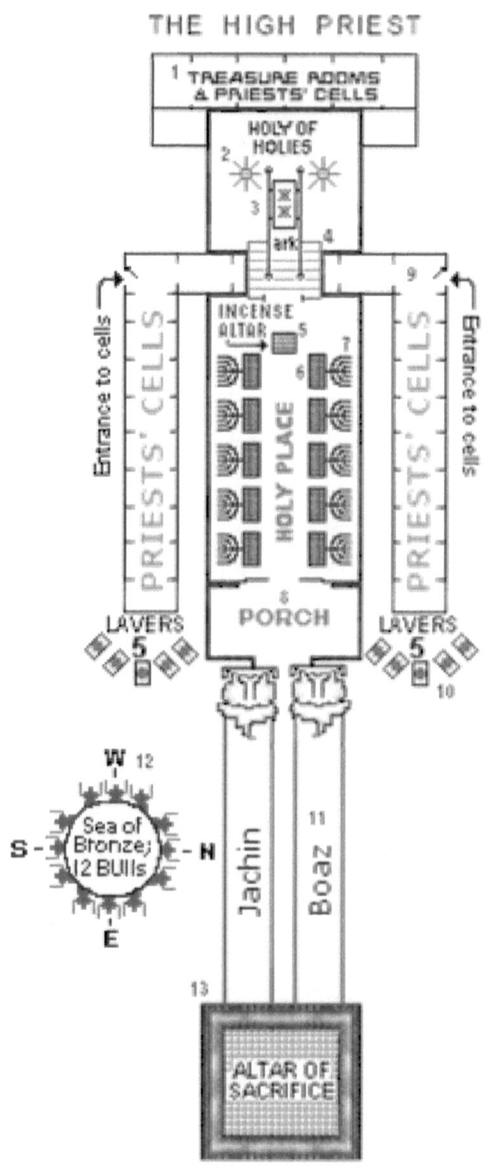
THE HIGH PRIEST
1 TREASURE ROOMS & PRIESTS' CELLS
HOLY OF HOLIES
2
3
ark
4
9
Entrance to cells
PRIESTS' CELLS
INCENSE ALTAR
5
6
7
HOLY PLACE
PRIESTS' CELLS
Entrance to cells
8
PORCH
LAVERS
5
LAVERS
5
10
W 12
Sea of Bronze; 12 BUlls
S
N
E
Jachin
11
Boaz
13
ALTAR OF SACRIFICE

When we open up the vertical legs we arrive at the picture on the right Now it is possible to identify the full Man in the Temple as follows: http://www.templesecrets.org/temple.html)
Here is how the High Priest's body and clothing correspond to the Temple and all its furniture:

The High Priest as Temple Man

At left is the Temple Floor Plan from the previous page now transformed into a figure of the Levite High Priest. Within the figure are 13 numbers, which are briefly explained below. All are in sequence except for nine (9).

1. **TREASURE ROOMS, PRIESTS' CELLS**, *west side* – Gold and silver bullion was kept in the Temple (I Kgs. 7:51) possibly in its western cells. These form the High Priest's turban (Heb., misnepet). The common priest's cap was more globular, like an inverted cup.

9. **PRIESTS' CELLS**, *south and north sides* – These form the arms. Only one entrance is named (I Kgs. 6:8) but Ezk. 41:11 includes a second. The entrances correspond to the onyx stones the High Priest wore on his left and right shoulders. Each was engraved with the names of six Israelite tribes, twelve names total, Ex. 28:9 -12.

2. **TWO LARGE STARS** – These are two10-cubit tall cherubs of gold plated olive wood (I Kgs. 6:23), they form Temple Man's eyes.

3. **THE ARK of the Covenant** – This was a gold plated chest with a solid gold lid topped by two small cherubs (small stars).The chest is his nose. Its *poles* were attached to its long sides rather than its short ones. They were drawn forward, I Kgs. 8:8, after the Ark was installed in the Holy of Holies and depict extended nostrils.

4. **STAIRWAY** – A short staircase led from the Holy Place to a slightly elevated Holy of Holies. The stairway is his neck/throat.

5. **INCENSE ALTAR** – This small gold plated altar (I Kgs. 6:22) is the heart. Its sweet-smelling smoke depicts prayer and the spiritual life.

6. **TABLES OF THE SHOWBREAD** – On these gold plated tables (I Kgs. 7:48) were bread and wine, symbolizing *flesh and blood,* i.e., the humanity of national Israel, the High Priest, and the Messiah.

7. **THE LAMPS** – These (II Chr. 4:7) provided light while portraying a Tree of Life. Their seven flames each stand for the seven days of Creation Week and also the seventy nations of the world. Light may symbolize divine knowledge and the spirit of God.

8. **THE PORCH** – This antechamber, the *ulam,* (I Kgs. 6:3, II Chr. 3:4) corresponds to the human pelvis (hips) and depicts procreation, or more specifically, birthing (parturition), because this is the area of the genital organs.

10, **TEN LAVERS** – Five bronze lavers were on the north and five on the south near the Porch. These signify the ten fingers of the hands. They were for washing off any residue of blood in the sacrificial meats (I Kgs. 7:38; II Chr. 4:6). They were mounted on wheeled carts and each laver held 40 baths of water.

11. **JACHIN, BOAZ** – These large bronze pillars by the Porch were named Jachin and Boaz (II Chr.3:17) and are the Temple Man's legs, Viewed standing, they portray two plants or trees and also the two kings, David and Solomon.

12. **SEA OF BRONZE, TWELVE BULLS** – This huge laver held 2000 or 3000 baths of water and was for the priests to wash their hands and feet (II Chr. 4:2). The laver depicts the basin of the Red Sea. Water too may depict God's spirit and knowledge but also conception, and union (devekut) with him. The twelve bulls (v.4) are the twelve tribes of Israel.

13. **THE SACRIFICIAL ALTAR** – This (II Chr. 4:1) is the Temple Man's feet, and also a king's square footstool. The Altar signifies election/separation, war and conquest (victory), atonement for sin, and national Israel's marriage to the Lord.

Tony also identifies the figure thus presented as the Metallic Messiah with the association of the predominant metal within each part.

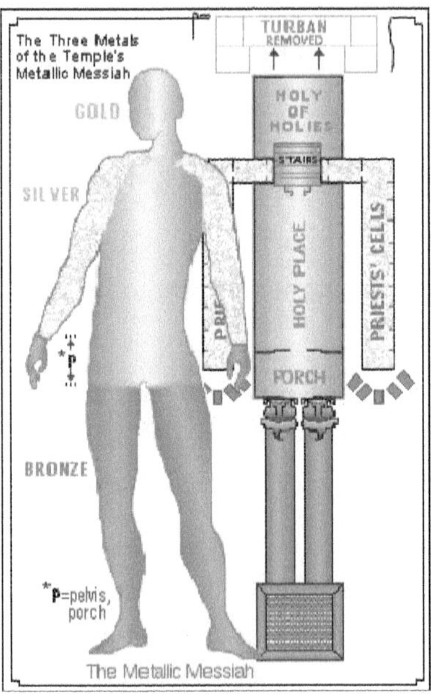

CHAPTER THREE

MALE AND FEMALE CREATED HE THEM

I . MALE AND FEMALE

"Then God said, "Let us make man in our image, after our likeness;; So God created man in his own image, in the image of God created he them, male and female he them." (Gen. 1:24-27) This was the creation of the sixth day. However abhorrent it may be for Semitic religion to conceive a consort to the deity, the picture here unequivocally declares that God had in him both male and female principles. Notice that this likeness of God is emphasized in the scripture several times. Four times the creation of man is mentioned in the Bible, and in all these four times this dualism is emphasized. (Gen. 1:27; 5:2; Mt. 19:4; Mk. 10:6) Gen. 5:1-2 reads; *"When God created man, he made him in the likeness of God, male and female he created them, and he blessed them and named them man, when they were created."* Thus the name man means the union of male and female. Male himself is not man, nor is he the likeness of God. Jesus also affirms this in his reference to the creation of man. *"Have you not read that he who made them from the beginning made them male and female." (Mt. 19:4; Mk:10:6)* This likeness is complete only in the union of male and female as Jesus goes on to show in Mt. 19:4-6. "For this reason a man shall leave his father and mother and be joined to his wife, and the two shall be one flesh." This of course is the conclusion based on *Gen. 2:24, "Therefore a man leaves his father and mother and cleaves to his wife and they become one flesh."*

However on the sixth day only Adam was created and we do not meet Eve until much later. The apparent implication is that like God, Adam held within him both the male and the female principles. This concept is further borne out in the story of creation of Adam and Eve. There is a world of difference between the creation of Adam and that of Eve. However much that God tried to find fellowship for Adam from the created beings of 'beasts of the field and birds of the air', he could not find a 'helper fit for him.' So an operation was performed and the female principle was separated from Adam as Eve; as a separate being.

Notice that Eve was not taken out of the dust - she was taken out of man. She was not given any breath of life. The spirit of Eve was the same spirit that was in Adam. "So the Lord God took one of his ribs and closed up its place with flesh; and the rib which the Lord had taken from the man, he made into a woman and brought her to the man." In the creation of man only two ingredients were used; dust from the ground and the breath of life. The joining of these two produced a qualitatively different property - a living soul. This is the personality, the self of man, which he develops as he interacts with the worlds both internal and external. But for Eve, only one ingredient was used - that was man. She was also a living soul. Evidently the operation was a splitting up of one whole into male and female. Adam recognized her and hence the need of leaving, cleaving and being one in order that he may be a complete man. Gen. 2:25 is of special value. "And the man and his wife were both naked, and were not ashamed." Thus for Adam and Eve, sex was a fulfillment of this oneness they were to experience.

II . MALE AND FEMALE PRINCIPLES IN GOD

Where is this male and female principle in God? It was conveniently covered up by the male dominated society. But those who read the Bible in its entirety cannot fail to see this.

We normally attribute three personalities to God - Gather, Son and the Holy Spirit. Son is identified with the Word of God, which incarnated on earth as Jesus, who nevertheless was the Son of Man even before his incarnation. He did appear himself as man to Abraham (Gen. 18:1-33) and to the elders of Israel (Gen. 24:9-11). The Holy Spirit is known to us in Her presence within us. How about Father? He has no form as is emphasized in the giving of the law to Moses (Deut. 4:15) But Jesus clearly addresses him as Father and later theology gives God a father image all through. (Mt. 5:16, 45,48; 6:4-32; 7:11,21; 10:29-33; 11:25-27; Rom. 1:7; 1 Cor. 8:6; 11:31; Gal. 1:2,3; 4:6 etc. a host of them) But this picture is not very clear in the Old Testament though Israel is often talked of as God's first born. Only in Malachi, there is a faint recognition of God as Father. (Mal. 1:6; 2:10)

Regarding the Word of God we read, "In the beginning was the Word, the Word was with God, and the Word was God. He was in the beginning with God; all things were made through Him." (Jn. 1:1-30)

In the Proverbs we meet a female figure - Wisdom- as the first creation or better as first of God's act. "The Lord created me at the beginning of his ...(this word is uncertain in the original), the first of his acts of old. I was beside him, like a master workman and I was daily his delight, rejoicing before him always, rejoicing in his inhabited world...." (Pro. 8:22-31) Wisdom was thus involved in the creation of the planner God. "The Lord by Wisdom founded the earth." (Pro. 3:19) The actual creation took place by the Word. But before that was the Wisdom which conceived the great plan of creation. Wisdom produced the Way, the Truth and the Life.

What exactly is the female principle in nature? It is the planning and the conceiving spirit, which produces changes and causes new creations. This description fits exactly the Holy Spirit, which as in the Proverbs as Wisdom was before creation, active with God as the conceiver and the giver of life. (Ja. 2:26; Gen. 1:2; 6:3) It is the spirit that gives life. In the first creation it was so. And so was it in the creation of the Word incarnation in Jesus and also in the creation of Adam. (Gen. 1:2; Lk. 1:35; Gen. 2:7) The same process takes place in the new creation of man in Christ Jesus. Here the body of Christ in conjunction with the Holy Spirit gives rise to the new creation man.

Thus in the biblical expression, there arose a separation of male and female principle from the God as the first act of God - the generation of Wisdom from the male-female absolute God. As long as God remained the unseparated unity, He remained non-creative Person - the Nirguna Brahman. Brahman without any property. As soon as the separation took place They became active and together began to create the Universe through the Word of God. The Nirguna became Saguna Brahman. This principle is also found in the creation of Adam. As long as Adam remained a unity of male-female, changes did not start, pro-creation did not start. This principle that female principle as the creative energy aspect is also found in other religions as well. Thus in Hindu mythology Sakthi is the consort of Siva and together in a dance the create the universe. Siva in essence is actually portrayed as Ardha-Narreswara - half woman, half man God. In all religions the principle of fertility is symbolized as a woman as in Venus, Adonis, Ishtar etc. This concept is so strongly embedded in the minds of man that even among large number of Christians, Jesus is helpless without Mother Mary. The introduction of Mother Mary as the Mother of God arose out of this inner urge of a female deity. The modern liberal address of "Our Mother who is in Heaven" etc. are a result of such deep-rooted understanding of man in their degenerate form.

In the creation of Church itself we can see a similar principle. As long as Jesus lived on the earth, he himself was a complete man. However no creation could take place in that state. In the cross, he was put to sleep and out of his body through the pierced wound came forth blood (the life carrier) and water (which is the spirit of creation - the water that cleanses and helps in creation Jn. 19:34) This blood was transferred into the life stream of the believers creating a new person in Church- who is the body of Christ and the bride of the Lamb. At the time of the Pentecost, the separation of Jesus was complete when the spirit was given to the church. Church therefore is the female aspect n- the creative aspect of Jesus. Her principal function is regeneration of additional cells, making each cell strong and grow into maturity that she may present herself as perfect before her groom. "Christ loved the church and gave himself up for her, that he might sanctify her, having cleansed

her by the washing of water with the word, that he might present the church to himself in splendor, without spot or wrinkle or any such thing, that she might be holy and without blemish." (Eph. 5:25-27)

III. REDEMPTION OF WOMAN

One of the immediate consequence of the fall of man was the alienation of man from woman. At the fall their eyes were opened and they realized that they were really two distinct, separate beings with separate bodies and separate personalities. Before the fall they had oneness of mind and they were one flesh. "Man and his wife were both naked and were not ashamed." Sex was their fulfillment of one-ness. But on the realization, their eyes were opened and they knew they were naked. They felt ashamed of their nakedness. So they sealed and expressed or declared their separateness by sewing fig leaves and making themselves aprons.

There was now a material covering for them, which said, "I am not you." It also created a separation from God and man and woman. Adam says, "

"I heard your voice, I was afraid, because I was naked." (Gen. 3:7,10) The self-consciousness hindered the relation ship of close fellowship of man with God. They saw themselves as two people with different interests and personalities needing to grow separately. This alienation aggravated in time through history each sex trying to assert themselves on the others. The greater muscular strength of man made him lord over the woman by brutal force. The woman tried to control man by her subtle senses. Pain and suffering, exploitation and aberrant management of persons and emotions continued through centuries. "Your desire shall be to your husband and he shall rule over you" (Gen. 3:16) The main point is this that this relation is a direct consequence of the fall. Any redemption of man should therefore involve the reinstatement of the relationship between man and wife before the fall.

In Jesus however the redemption of man is accomplished, but is not fully realized. "Christ has redeemed us from the curse of the law, having become a curse for us." Gal. 3:13) Thus in Christ women are liberated and made equal with man as coheirs to the Kingdom of God. "There is neither Jew nor Greek, there is neither slave or free, there is neither male or female; for we are all one is Christ Jesus." (Gal. 1:28) "In like manner, you husbands live with your wife, according to knowledge, giving honor unto wife, as unto a weaker vessel, and as being heirs together of the grace of life......" (1 Pe. 3:7)

We see this equality in Jesus' dealing with women. It is true He did not choose women in the twelve disciples because of the social and cultural constraints of that period.. But many women were very close to Jesus, probably closer than many in the twelve. (See Luke 8:1-3) Apparently women took Jesus very seriously and believed him more than many of his closer disciples themselves. None of his teachings differentiates man and woman. On the other hand he emphasized the equality of woman and man in marriage. Even his disciples were surprised with his teachings about monogamy and chastity of man as well as women. (Mt. 15:38) Large number of women attended his meetings. (Mt. 15:38) During the period of Jesus' agony on the cross, it was the women who faithfully stayed with him, when all the disciples were scattered with fear. (Mt. 27:55; Mk. 15:40; Jn. 19:25-26)

There were five Marys in Jesus' close circle. The question of who supported the mission of Jesus is partially at least answered by Luke, which indicates the part played by women in His ministry. (Lk. 8:3)

Thus a full redemption of man should involve a complete reinstatement of man in relation to the sex. This is exemplified in Jesus' relation with the Church. The ultimate ideal is the relation of Father with the Holy Spirit. "In the Lord women is not independent of man, nor man of women; for as woman was made from man, so man is now born from women. All things are from God.' This completes the shadow of Trinity with man (1 Cor. 11: 11-12)

Thus looking forward to this ideal, Paul advises thus in Ephesians, "Therefore be imitators of God.....walk in love..... Be subject to one another out of reverence for Christ. Wives be subject to your husbands, as to the Lord. For the husband is the head of the wife as Christ is the head of the Church, his body, and is himself her savior. As the church is subject to Christ, so let wives also subject in everything to their husbands. Husbands love your wives, as Christ loved the Church and gave himself up for her......Even so husbands should love their wives as their own bodies. He who loves his wife, loves himself. For no man ever hates his own flesh, but nourishes it and cherishes it, as Christ to Church, because we are members of His body. "For this reason a man shall leave his father and mother and be joined to his wife, and the two shall become one flesh." This mystery is a profound one, and I am saying that it refers to Christ and the Church." (Eph. 5:21-32) So also Peter advises (1 Pe. 3:7) Notice Peter's emphasis on the joint heirship of man and woman to the abundant life. Abundant life cannot be attained with broken family relation. He goes on to say that no prayers can be answered by God if the family is separated and women are not honored as coheirs. Abundant life is a joint account obtainable only by both parties counter signing. Thus family is a vital component in the full redemption of man and to his entry into the Kingdom of God.

Satan's front line attack today is in the family as it had been in the Garden of Eden. Two types of heresies are rampant today. One extreme is the teaching of licentiousness - sex as a means of god-realization without love. These gurus propose indiscriminate sex as though it will create love and unity

."But false prophets also are among the people , just as there will be false teachers among you, who will bring in destructive heresies, even denying the Master who bought them, bringing upon themselves swift destruction. And many will follow their licentiousness, and because of them the way of the truth will be reviled. (2 Pe. 2:1-2) There is then the other extreme as Paul warns in 1 Tim. 4:3) "Now the spirit expressly says that in the later times one will depart from the truth by heeding to deceitful spirit and

doctrines of demons,.....who forbid marriage and enjoin abstinence..." Kundalini Yoga attempts both these practices and was very prevalent in Indian culture during the period of Independence.

We thus look forward to the glory that Jesus has given us as expressed in his Priestly prayer Jn. 17:20-25 "....that they may be one; even as thou, Father, art in me, and I in thee, that they also may be in us...even as we are one, I in them and thou in me, that they may be come perfectly one....."

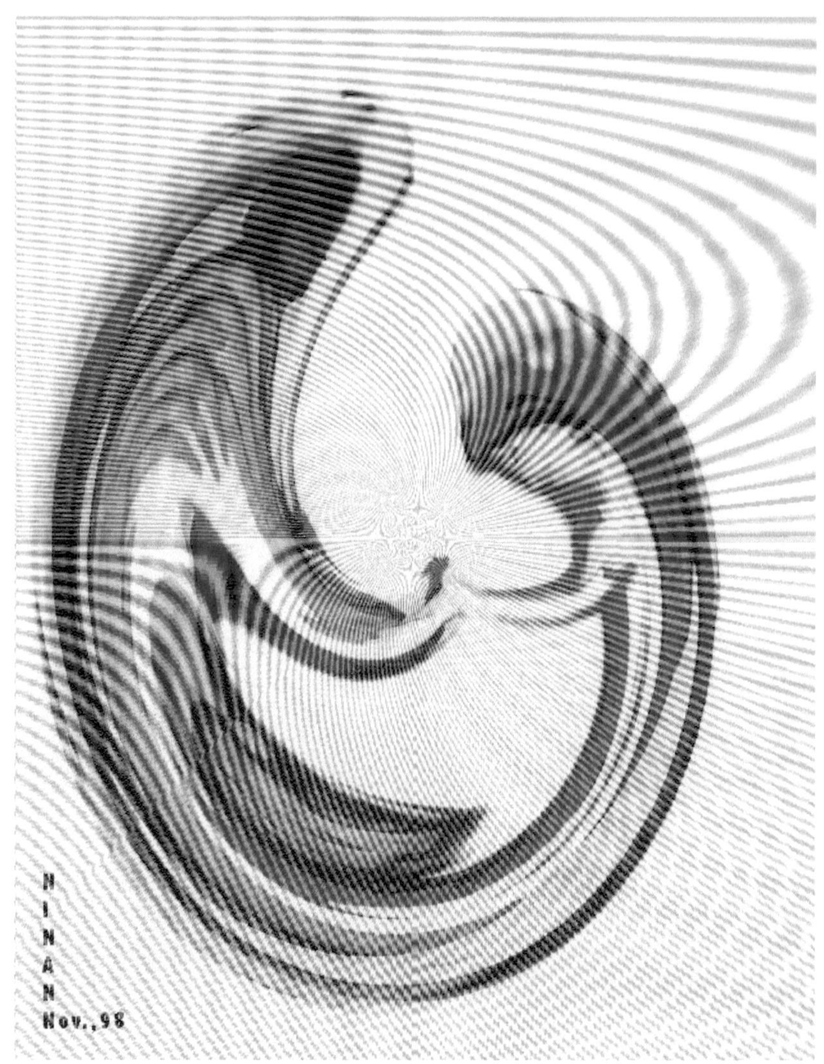

Male and Female Created He them.

CHAPTER FOUR

SCALAR AND VECTOR MODELS OF MAN

I .TWO SPIRIT SCALAR MODEL

We now consider a very familiar model of man which has been in use widely for evangelization.

NATURAL MAN

This model considers man in the world who is unregenerate as man with his ego on the throne of his soul and the cross outside of him. He is alien to the kingdom of heaven. He has the sinful nature within them. Unregenerate man is sinful by nature. He cannot understand spiritual things nor can he know God.

1Cor. 2:14 The man without the Spirit does not accept the things that come from the Spirit of God, for they are foolishness to him, and he cannot understand them, because they are spiritually discerned.

Jude 19 These are the men who divide you, who follow mere natural instincts and do not have the Spirit.

Gal. 5:19-21 The acts of the sinful nature are obvious: sexual immorality, impurity and debauchery; idolatry and witchcraft; hatred, discord, jealousy, fits of rage, selfish ambition, dissensions, factions and envy; drunkenness, orgies, and the like. I warn you, as I did before, that those who live like this will not inherit the kingdom of God.

Rom. 1:29-32 They have become filled with every kind of wickedness, evil, greed and depravity. They are full of envy, murder, strife, deceit and malice. They are gossips, slanderers, God-haters, insolent, arrogant and boastful; they invent ways of doing evil; they disobey their parents; they are senseless, faithless, heartless, and ruthless. Although they know God's righteous decree that those who do such things deserve death, they not only continue to do these very things but also approve of those who practice them.

1Cor. 6:9 -11 Do you not know that the wicked will not inherit the kingdom of God? Do not be deceived: Neither the sexually immoral nor idolaters nor adulterers nor male prostitutes nor homosexual offenders nor thieves nor the greedy nor drunkards nor slanderers nor swindlers will inherit the kingdom of God. And that is what some of you were. But you were washed, you were sanctified, you were justified in the name of the Lord Jesus Christ and by the Spirit of our God.

Col. 3:5-6 Put to death, therefore, whatever belongs to your earthly nature: sexual immorality, impurity, lust, evil desires and greed, which is idolatry. Because of these, the wrath of God is coming.

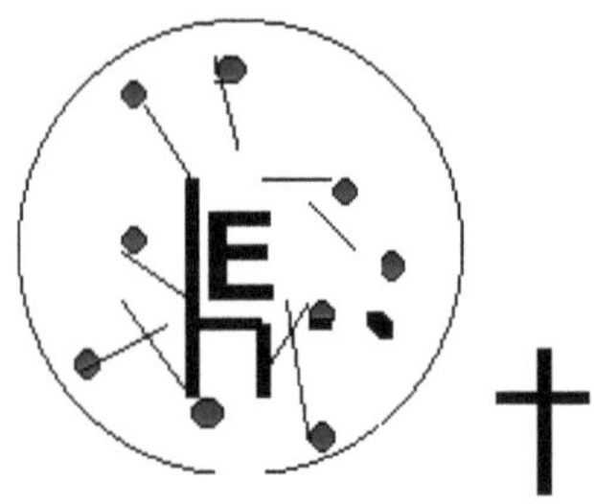

Fig 1

UNREGENERATE MAN

His own ego is inside. But he has not got the spirit of God in him . He is not born again

CARNAL CHRISTIAN

This is the man who has accepted Jesus as his savior. He now becomes a new creature - new creation in Christ Jesus. But he is still controlled by his ego, which is on the throne. He is not controlled by the Holy spirit. As a result his actions are still pulled apart by different desires and in still similar to the sensual unregenerate man.

Col 3:6-9: You used to walk in these ways, in the life you once lived. But now you must rid yourselves of all such things as these: anger, rage, malice, slander, and filthy language from your lips. Do not lie to each other, since you have taken off your old self with its practices and have put on the new self, which is being renewed in knowledge in the image of its Creator.

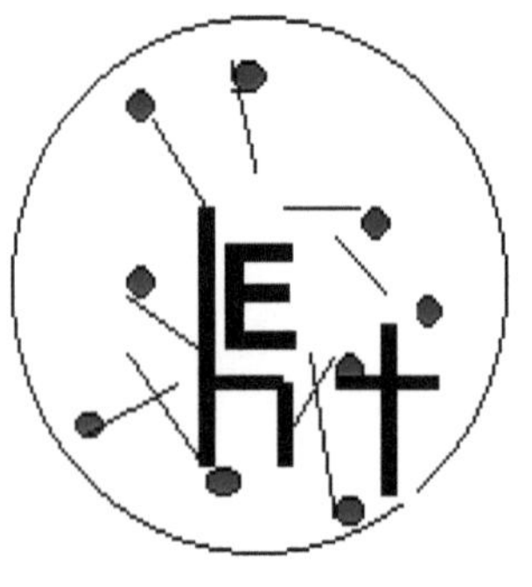

Fig 2

REGENERATED BABES

CARNAL MAN

The spirit of God is in him, but his own ego is on the throne. New creature resurrected from death in trespasses and sins

1Cor. 3:1 Brothers, I could not address you as spiritual but as worldly --mere infants in Christ.

2Cor. 5:17 -18 Therefore, if anyone is in Christ, he is a new creation; the old has gone, the new has come! All this is from God, who reconciled us to himself through Christ and gave us the ministry of reconciliation:

SPIRIT CONTROLLED CHRISTIAN

The spirit controlled spiritual man is one who has Christ on the throne of his soul and the spirit controls all his desires so that it is in consonance with the word of God.

1Cor. 15:44 -46 it is sown a natural body, it is raised a spiritual body. If there is a natural body, there is also a spiritual body. So it is written: "The first man Adam became a living being" ; the last Adam, a life-giving spirit.

The spiritual did not come first, but the natural, and after that the spiritual.

Gal. 6:1 Brothers, if someone is caught in a sin, you who are spiritual should restore him gently. But watch yourself, or you also may be tempted.

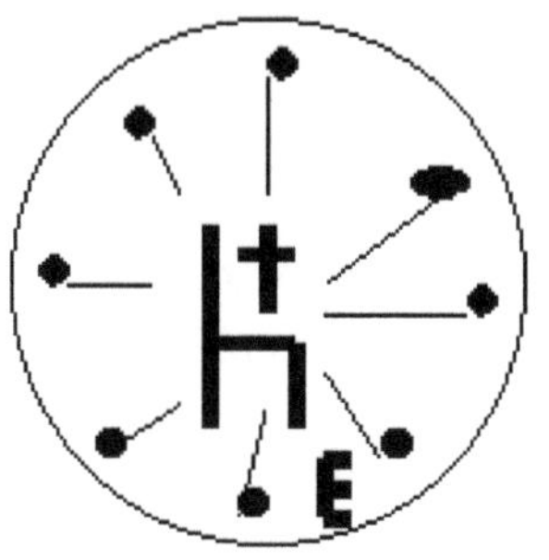

fig 3

Spirit Controlled Christian

Every action is controlled by the Holy spirit

Eph. 4:22 -24 You were taught, with regard to your former way of life, to put off your old self, which is being corrupted by its deceitful desires; to be made new in the attitude of your minds; and to put on the new self, created to be like God in true righteousness and holiness.

However this model is too simplistic and the transition from carnal Spirit controlled life is a long process where each step involves Lower animal passions being continuously crucified until we grow into the full image of Jesus Christ.

Rom. 8:12 -13 Therefore, brothers, we have an obligation --but it is not to the sinful nature, to live according to it. For if you live according to the sinful nature, you will die; but if by the Spirit you put to death the misdeeds of the body, you will live,

Gal. 2:20 I have been crucified with Christ and I no longer live, but Christ lives in me. The life I live in the body, I live by faith in the Son of God, who loved me and gave himself for me.

Gal. 5:24 Those who belong to Christ Jesus have crucified the sinful nature with its passions and desires.

Eph. 2:22 And in him you too are being built together to become a dwelling in which God lives by his Spirit.

Col. 3:5-10 Put to death, therefore, whatever belongs to your earthly nature: sexual immorality, impurity, lust, evil desires and greed, which is idolatry. Because of these, the wrath of God is coming. You used to walk in these ways, in the life you once lived. But now you must rid yourselves of all such things as these: anger, rage, malice, slander, and filthy language from your lips. Do not lie to each other, since you have taken off your old self with its practices and have put on the new self, which is being renewed in knowledge in the image of its Creator.

Rom. 8:5-16 Those who live according to the sinful nature have their minds set on what that nature desires; but those who live in accordance with the Spirit have their minds set on what the Spirit desires. The mind of sinful man is death, but the mind controlled by the Spirit is life and peace; ...... For if you live according to the sinful nature, you will die; but if by the Spirit you put to death the misdeeds of the body, you will live, because those who are led by the Spirit of God are sons of God. For you did not receive a spirit that makes you a slave again to fear, but you received the Spirit of sonship. And by him we cry, "Abba, Father." The Spirit himself testifies with our spirit that we are God's children.

Gal. 5:16 So I say, live by the Spirit, and you will not gratify the desires of the sinful nature.

This could be represented as a filling of the Holy Spirit as we open up areas of our lives to the Holy spirit in day today life. Progressive Sanctification then leads to Christ likeness.

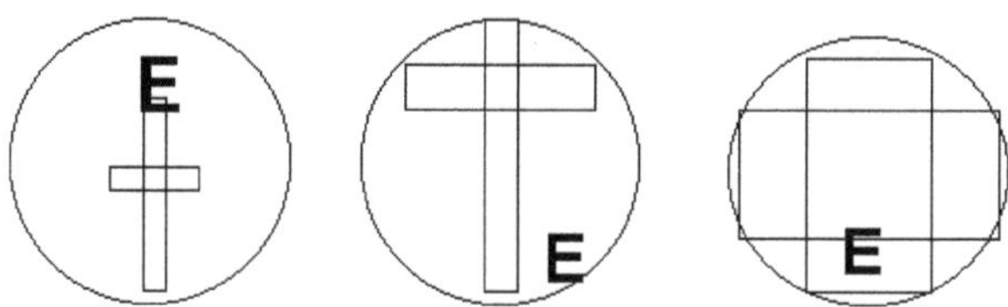

Fig 4
Progressive Sanctification

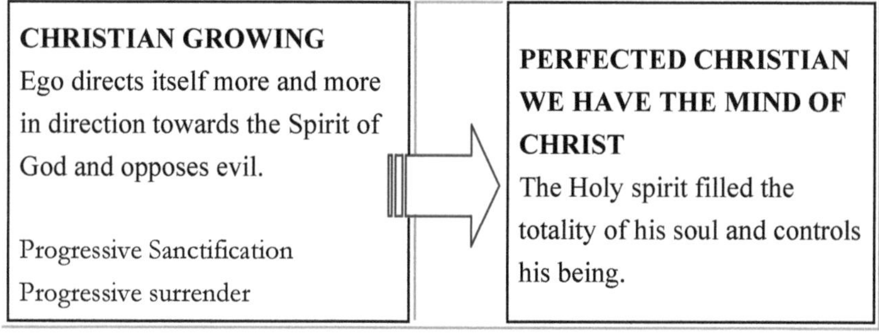

The same concept of how the Spirit of God fills the entire human dimensions of Spirit, Soul and Body from the inside is beautifully expressed in the following figure, which speaks for itself.

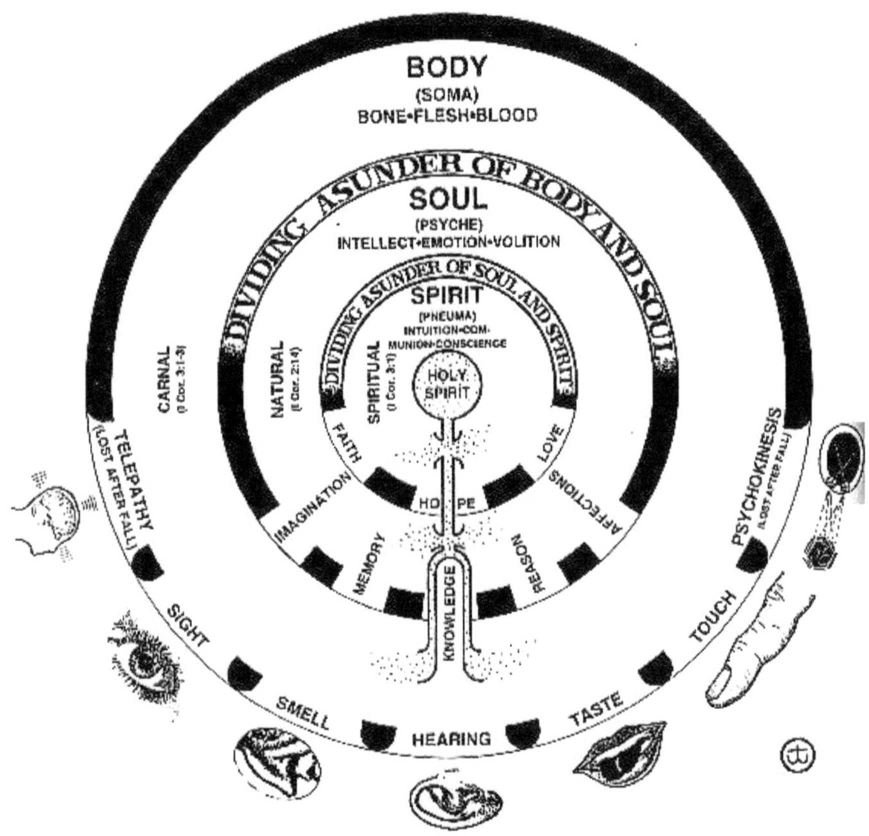

http://www.ldolphin.org/unruh/planet/ch8ph.html

II .THREE SPIRIT VECTOR MODEL

There is another model that can be developed on the basis of the forces acting on the human soul in their life trajectory. A direct statement on these three forces are given in 1 Corinthians as below:

1Cor. 2:10-12 but God has revealed it to us by his Spirit. The Spirit searches all things, even the deep things of God. For who among men knows the thoughts of a man except the man's spirit within him? In the same way no one knows the thoughts of God except the Spirit of God. Now we have received not the spirit of this world, but the Spirit, which is from God, that we might understand the gifts bestowed on us by God.

These verses in Paul's analysis of man in the world gives us three distinct spirits that exist in the spiritual universe of existence. We are now talking about the spiritual dimension where the real action is.

1. The Spirit who is from God, (Holy Spirit ,Spirit of God)

John 4:24 God is spirit, and his worshipers must worship him in spirit and in truth."

We have seen earlier that one of the Trinity is Holy spirit. God gives this Holy spirit into the hearts of those who believe in him.

2. The spirit of man

God created the spirit of man within him. It is a force that gives man his direction, purpose and power. Spirit of man is the life giving spirit within man, it controls him.

Prov. 18:14 A man's spirit sustains him in sickness, but a crushed spirit who can bear?

Isa. 57:16 the spirit of man would grow faint before me-- the breath of man that I have created.

1Cor. 2:11 For who among men knows the thoughts of a man except the man's spirit within him? In the same way no one knows the thoughts of God except the Spirit of God.

This spirit can be weak, strong or faint. It has variable strength depending on the growth of the person. Each person is a vector in with magnitude and direction in the plane of existence.

The fundamental immutable reality is God. Hence man must be compared and related with God. Sin and righteousness is definable only in terms of God. It has no other meaning possible. Evil was not created, because a good God cannot create evil. Evil is definable only in terms of a moral beings direction with respect to God. That is what we have done in this vector definition. This property we call Righteousness. Negative righteousness is then evil. In this universe each being is either righteous or evil in charge. The charge of the nonliving is zero because it does not have a spirit. A living being can have a charge zero if it does not have a component in the direction of God. He is neither good nor bad.

2Pet. 1:4 the corruption in the world caused by evil desires.

James 4:4 You adulterous people, don't you know that friendship with the world is hatred toward God? Anyone who chooses to be a friend of the world becomes an enemy of God.

1John 2:15 -16 Do not love the world or anything in the world. If anyone loves the world, the love of the Father is not in him. For everything in the world --the cravings of sinful man, the lust of his eyes and the boasting of what he has and does --comes not from the Father but from the world.

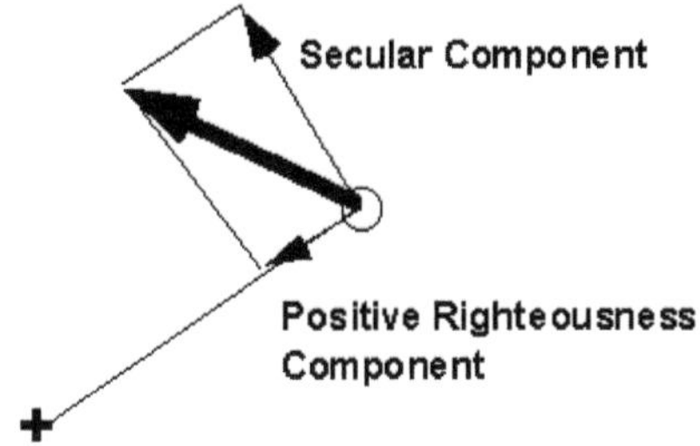

Fig. 5
Righteous Being or Positive Righteous Charge

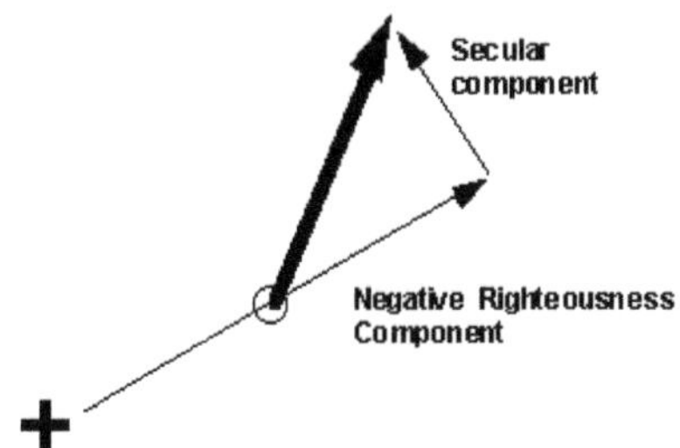

Fig. 6
Devil or Unrighteous Being or Negative Righteous Charge

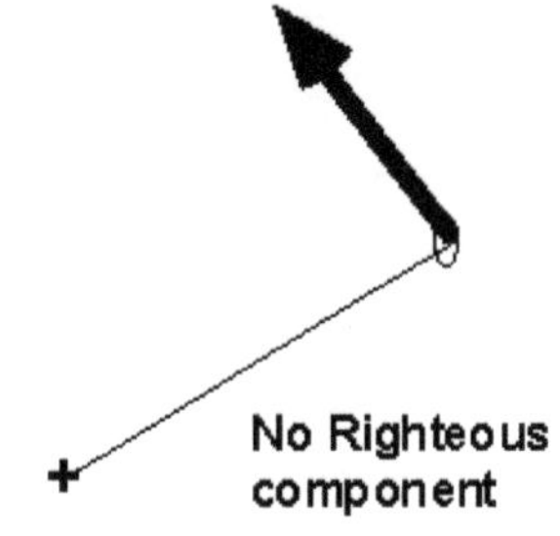

Fig. 7

This being has zero righteous component i.e. Secular Being or Zero Righteousness Charge.

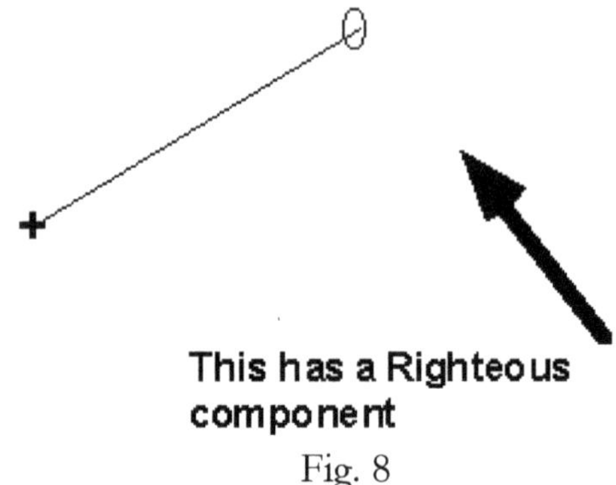

Fig. 8

Though this vector has the same direction and magnitude as in figure 3, this vector do have a + ve component in the direction of + It is the position of the being with respect the God that makes the difference. This explains the principle of situational ethics. An act may be righteous or secular depending on the state of the person who performs it, where he is in relation to God. So here we have a situation where not only the magnitude, and direction but also the position matters.

3.. The spirit of the world

The world is filled with creatures with free will. Each being is a vector in the space. The direction of the vector may be defined in terms of the reference point, which is unchangeable- which is God's Spirit. The direction of the vectors can then be defined + or - depending on whether the vector has a positive component in the direction of God point or a negative component. the spirit, which has a positive component towards God, is called righteous and those that have negative component is called unrighteous or evil. Such a person is often called a devil.

Christianity rejects the idea of a negative God i.e. Satan as the antithesis of God. The Zoroastrian (Parsee) religion and most of the religions of the Middle East at the time of Israel believed in a polarized, equal and fighting good and bad gods. God is a good God - if the term can be applied to God. He did not create evil. Evil is not a physical reality. It is a moral reality arising out of the actions of a free moral agent. Man and other creatures of God created with a free will generates evil because they move away from God and follow other interests contrary to the purposes of God. This is the source of evil. Such an agent whether man or spirit, terrestrial or alien may be called the devil. There are many devils and many Antichrists in this world. The moral agent moving towards God and acting as a free agent is righteous. They are saints. But they need not necessarily be in consonance with God nor targeted directly on Him. These spirit beings form a cloud of righteous beings, unrighteous beings and secular beings. This cloud is similar in distribution as electrostatic distribution of charges. In the presence of God the righteous will move towards God and the unrighteous away from God. Hence at any instant there will be distribution of these with concentration of the righteous around and near God and concentration of unrighteous away from God. A polarization has taken place. We can replace this hazy field of distributed + and - by two centers of masses; + which is God and - which we may designate as - and call Satan.

1John 5:19 We know that we are children of God, and that the whole world is under the control of the evil one.

Thus Satan is an apparent personality- not real. It is really of title. It is the title of a being who becomes the center of mass or center of attraction of the evil beings. It is a power source of all evil. A better definition can be made in the terminology of dynamics as the sink. Where God is the source and the generator of righteousness, Satan is the sink of righteousness. He is the source of evil but not the only generator of it. In practice the evilest may be termed as such. This apparent negative charge cloud provided by the negative charges by polarization is called the spirit of the world.

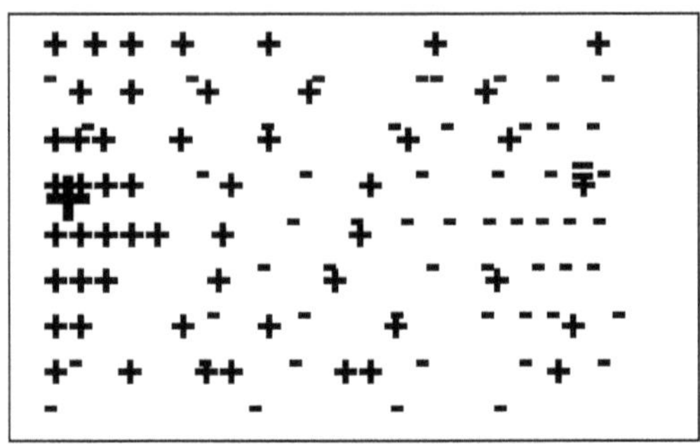

Fig. 9 The Spirits that are in this World
Polarization of Righteous and Unrighteous Spirits

Eph. 6:12 For our struggle is not against flesh and blood, but against the rulers, against the authorities, against the powers of this dark world and against the spiritual forces of evil in the heavenly realms.

Notice the plural used in these - rulers, authorities, powers etc. The power of these lie in hollow and deceptive philosophy, and human traditions:

Col. 2:8 See to it that no one takes you captive through hollow and deceptive philosophy, which depends on human tradition and the basic principles of this world rather than on Christ.

Col. 2:20 Since you died with Christ to the basic principles of this world,

1John 4:3 but every spirit that does not acknowledge Jesus is not from God. This is the spirit of the antichrist, which you have heard is coming and even now is already in the world.

1John 4:4-5 You, dear children, are from God and have overcome them, because the one who is in you is greater than the one who is in the world. They are from the world and therefore speak from the viewpoint of the world, and the world listens to them. (Plural indicates who is a plurality personified as he in the previous sentence.)

2John 7 Many deceivers, who do not acknowledge Jesus Christ as coming in the flesh, have gone out into the world. Any such person is the deceiver and the antichrist.

If we now consider a being placed in this field three vectors will be acting. These are:

1. Attraction to God (Spirit of God because of the induced Spirit within him.)

2. Attraction to Evil (Spirit that is in the world. This is because he is part of the field)

3. Self - Ego or self will (Spirit of Man)

The human spirit's force may be weak or strong and may direct in any direction. It is these that make the position of the particular person. The ultimate aim of every man is to be like Jesus.

Eph. 4:13 until we all reach unity in the faith and in the knowledge of the Son of God and become mature, attaining to the whole measure of the fullness of Christ.

In our model it means that man should reach ultimately the +. It is the trajectory of man that is determined by the three forces in this space. The dynamics of the motion is totally controlled by the spirit of the man concerned. The freedom and the responsibility is totally his. To steer himself through to reach the ultimate source he need to change directions, he needs to change the magnitude of his force depending on the position he finds. Human realization is a dynamic process and not static. That is what makes life interesting.

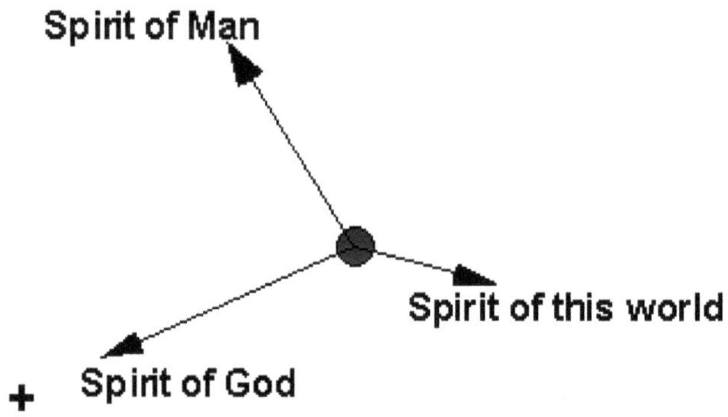

Fig 10
Three Forces on man

These three spirits are related to the three offices ordained by God, viz. Prophet, Priest and King. These offices were ordained in a fallen world as a method of redemption process.

The function of the Priest is

1. to act as a conservative force and

2. to act as judge in the society to impose justice,

3. to propitiate for the sins of the world, and

4. to act as a healers.

Leviticus provides detailed functions of the Priests. Basically we consider Priests as those who offer regular ceremonial services and provide a stable system. As such they offer atonement and sacrifices for the sins and pronounce pardon. But Priests judged between people, and acted as medicine men. The conservative function provided by the secular component of the spirit of Man and the execution of judgment, healing, and atonement are provided by the components that are along the spirit opposing the spirit of the World and those along the direction of the Spirit from God. Thus Man's spirit represents the Priest. We should note that since man is a free agent the spirit can act as an anti-Priest in unrighteous spirits. In an unrighteous spirit the conservative component is still there. But it will judge against Godly principles and introduce injustice, nullify atonement and introduce sickness, faster decay and death.

The function of the Prophet on the other hand is :

1. to reveal the nature of God through history as it is unfolded. He is the voice of God, the declarer and the announcer for God.

2. to interpret the principles of righteousness in the context of the state of man and society- a watchman one who shows the transgressions and sins. He is the interpreter and expositor of the Law.

3. to bring Man nearer to God - an exhorter

4. to reveal the future. This arises only as a natural consequence of the actions. But the prophet is not really a fortuneteller.

Evidently this is done by the Spirit from God. In the Old Testament Period, the Holy Spirit came on the prophets and they prophesied. In the New Testament, the Holy Spirit abides within man once he is saved by the cross.

Kingship relies on Power and Lordship. Thus the Spirit of this world is described by Paul as Principalities and Powers. This is what is represented in the Spirit of this world. Human Kingship is a perversion or reversion of the Kingship concept of God. Power and authority in the Kingdom of

God is directly related to Servant hood. In Jesus' concept the greatest in the Kingdom of God is to be the servant of all. When Father gave all power into his hands Jesus took water and began to wash the feet of his disciples. Earthly kingship is the negation of the Kingship of God. That is what God told Samuel when Israel asked for a King like other nations.

As long as the Spirit of Man vector is in the side towards God , he i.e. a righteous man will perform three functions: The component opposing the Spirit of World will provide:

1. Opposition to the Spirit of the World - i.e. Kingship of the World

2. Atonement for the sins of the world

The Secular component will provide

3. The conservation so that he may not change too fast under any force making it impossible to adjust for the variations.

However when the vector component opposing the Spirit of this world is more than what is required for the atonement of sins he will miss the target of God. This case is shown in fig.11 This is because he will be then acting as God. For this reason, every High Priest was required to make an atonement for himself before he took the sin offering for others.

The model offers several interesting features:

1. In this case for example

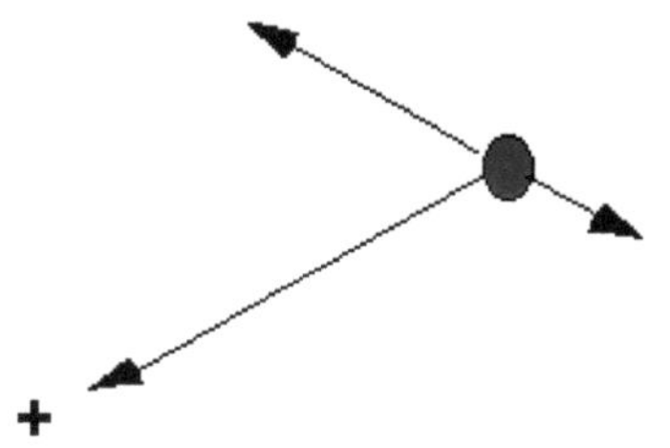

Secular tendencies are strong enough that he will miss reaching the target.

Fig 11
This is the picture of a righteous man. The net resultant is away from the - but directed not at +. He will therefore miss the target. He is still a sinner, because sin is missing the target.

One important result is that the best way to reach God is by

1. Neutralize the spirit in the world with human spirit. Oppose the devil. Stronger reaction will make you to miss the target. Weaker self will make you move away.

2. Yield to the Spirit of God completely them.

James 4:7 Submit yourselves, then, to God. Resist the devil, and he will flee from you.
Eph. 4:27 and do not give the devil a foothold.
1Pet. 5:8 Be self-controlled and alert. Your enemy the devil prowls around like a roaring lion looking for someone to devour

The following vector diagram illustrates this fact.

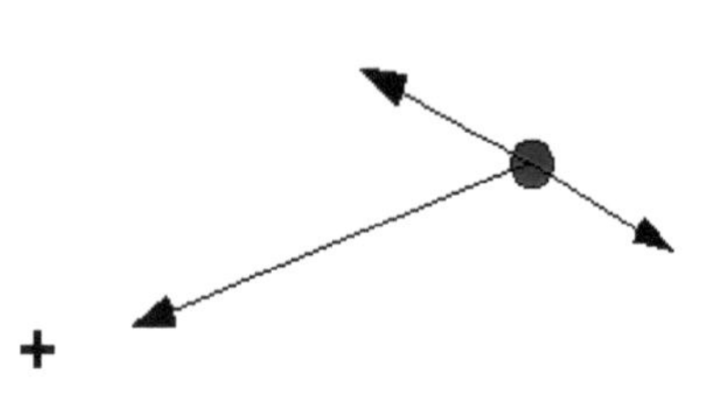

Fig. 12

Totally controlled by the Holy Spirit.

Resist the devil- Spirit of man opposes and destroys the evil tendencies. The consequent total submission to the Holy Spirit leads him on target to God.

If the spirit pulls against the spirit of the world more than neutralization it will be as in fig. 11 leading to miss the mark i.e. to sin. That is why Paul warns against the excessive Puritanism.

Col. 2:21-23 "Do not handle! Do not taste! Do not touch!"? These are all destined to perish with use, because they are based on human commands and teachings. Such regulations indeed have an appearance of wisdom, with their self-imposed worship, their false humility and their harsh treatment of the body, but they lack any value in restraining sensual indulgence.

Here again notice that as he moves, he need to readjust both the direction and magnitude of his spirit force, and this is a continuous process.

3. A person may be far away from God, living in the midst of sinners, yet he may be counted righteous. If he persevere he will find Christ.

Fig 13

Here is a man far away from God, surrounded by evil, but he moves away from the evil towards +, though not directly. Missiologically speaking most of the people who have never heard of Jesus fall into this category. they can be reached for Christ and must be.

4. Similarly a man may be very near to God and may be unrighteous. He will eventually fall away from Christ.

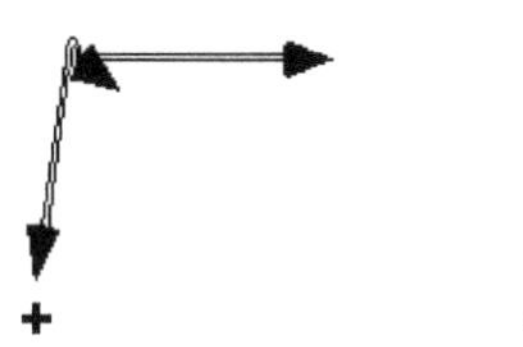

Fig. 14

This is the opposite case. Here is a man close to God, but his ego pulls him away from God. There are many great Christians, who are led away by their vanities and worldly attractions to fall away. According to Hebrews they cannot be reclaimed.

What other deductions can we make from this?
What are their missiological implications?
What is the difference between a Christian and a non-Christian ?
Who is a Christian?
Can we expect good from non-Christians? Can we call them Christians?
What is our responsibility in this world?

CHAPTER FIVE

THE KABBALISTIC ANTHROPOLOGY : ADAM KADAMON AND THEOSIS

(Heb 2:11) "For he who sanctifies and those who are sanctified have all one origin. That is why he is not ashamed to call them brethren."

Kabala is the mystic tradition within Judaism. Kabala (Qabala) means "what has been handed down", the "faith that has been handed down once and for all" i.e. Tradition. In the Indian tradition it corresponds to Smriti or what is remembered. The word Kabala is derived from the Hebrew "kabel" which means "to receive." Kabbah (Muslim Kabbah came from it) means revelation. Kabala simply means revelations of God. It originally applied only to the Oral Law "received" after the destruction of the Second Temple, in the form of the Talmud. The idea is that just as there is a written scripture the "Torah", (*Pentateuch* to which commentaries were added such as *Talmud*, *Mishnah*, etc.), there is also a transmitted interpretation on the hidden secrets within the torah. This is handed down by word of mouth and is known as Kabala. Since the dispersion of the Jews all over the world, attempts have been made to write these down. Though it was fully developed in the Middle Ages, the first seeds of a mystical trend began to emerge in the talmudic literature, written well after the destruction of the Second Temple--from 150 A.D. to 600 A.D.

One of the problems with tradition is that it is prone to corruption and variations with time and space. Anything that is transmitted by word of mouth is bound to get corrupted by additions and interpretations and interpolations. Hence we have varying traditions in it. Thus there are several variations in the Kabalistic anthropology.

The Cosmic Adam – First Man, who is the first appearance of comprehensible reality that emanated from the incomprehensible Ultimate Reality of Godhead, represents Cosmos. In the early Christian thinking this represents the Son - the word who became flesh. In Kabala He is represented as a Man who exists in four dimensions. A reflection of this is seen in Rg Veda Purusha Suktha. (which came into existence during the second and third century AD under the influence of St.Thomas Churches that existed all over India) as the 90th Suktam of its 10th mandalam, with 16 mantrams. It describes Parama Purusha, Purushottama, Narayana, in his form as the ViraaT Purusha. - the source of all creation.

This great being Purusha has thousands of heads,
Thousands of eyes, and thousands of legs.
He manifests the world.
He stands beyond the measures.

Out of the sacrifice of this Purusha came the cosmos. Love means sacrifice. Out of love He created. All creations involves love and that involves sacrifice. There is a cross in all creation.

The whole creation is this Purusha,
that which was and that which is to be
Act 17:28 for 'In him we live and move and have our being';

This Purusha exists in four dimensions.
There are various beings in all the four dimensions which form the cosmic Purusha.

The Four Worlds of the Kabballah:

Sepher Yetzirah or the "Book of Creation." is the canonical text for the later Kabalistic movement which developed the workings and the origin of the universe. It described the sefirot or "emanations," the ten so-called "manifestations of God." .

An understanding of the Kabballah traditions gives the background information for the Biblical understanding of Cosmos and God. It talks about four worlds of existence that have emanated from Ein-Sof (the unknowable God) who dwells in darkness and who cannot be known. These are:

1. ATZILUTH

The Divine or Archetypal World.
The ***Yod*** of Tetragrammaton.
Secret Name: ***AB*** - Father
Element - Fire.

Atziluth is the highest plane of Creation. It is the well spring from which everything emerges. It is difficult for the Human mind to comprehend the workings or the ideas that are associated with such high realms of consciousness. The very essence of pure thought and to some extent the very mind of the Creator may be glimpsed briefly in the Realm of Atziluth.

Atziluth is administered by the Highest of Beings - the Cherubim. They would appear to be extremely close to the Mind of God, in fact closer than any others. Thought and is the backdrop for all that is. Without the Divine influence of Atziluth nothing is Atziluth represents the ideas that are in the mind of God.

Atzilut, the "World of Emanation" or "Nearness (to the Godhead)", also called the Image and the Heavenly man (*Adam Kadmon*), is the Divine Reality; the Sefirot or attributes of the Godhead. They are the direct emanation from the En Sof, and hence most intimately connected to the absolute Deity, perfect and immutable. [C.D.Ginsburg, S.A.Cook, "Kabbalah", *Encyclopeadia Britannica*, 11th ed. 1911, vol xv, pp.620-1].

The Sefirot are arranged in three pillars, the Pillar of Mercy (Hesed) on the left, the Pillar of Judgment or Severity (Gevurah) on the right, and the Pillar of Balance or Compassion or Beauty (Tifaret) in the middle; which together constitute the Divine supervision of the lower worlds

2. BRIAH

The Archangelic or Creative world.
The First Hek of Tetragrammaton.
Secret Name: *Seg*
Element - Water.

The world of Briah is the world of early Creation. The Archangels form the governing and ordering body. Briah is most commonly associated with the Element of Water. It is in Briah that the Mighty Archangels appear to establish the Will of God. Briah is where the plans are made and the "blueprints" are drawn. Briah, the "World of Creation" is also called "the Throne" ten sefirot being further from the En Sof then the sefirot of the universe of Atzilut, are of a more limited potency, although their substance is still of the purest nature and without any admixture of matter. The angel Metatron inhabits this world. He constitutes the world of pure spirit and is the garment of *Shaddai*, i.e. the visible manifestation of the Divine. He governs the visible world, preserves its harmony, and is head of myriads of angels [C.D.Ginsburg, S.A.Cook, *Kabbalah*, p.621].

The world of Beriah is described in the Zohar as consisting of seven higher heavens or firmaments which emanate from the seven lower sefirot of Atzilut, and are beyond the traditional seven heavens to which the stars and planets are fixed [Paul Krzok, "The Cosmological Structure of the Zohar", p.32 The Hermetic Journal, no.20, Summer 1983)]. This is also the world of the angels centered around the throne of God.

In the Lurianic tradition this is the world where the tzimtzum is first felt, and hence individual beings are able to exist. (Jacob Immanuel Schochet, *Mystical Concepts in Hassidism* Kehot Publication Society, Brooklyn New York, 1979, p.110)

Beriah is identified with the Sefirah Binah this is region from which the divine soul (*Neshamah*) is derived.

3. YETZIRAH (Formation)

Olam ha-Yetzirah.
The Angelic or Formative world.
The World of thought.
The Vau of Tettragrammaton.
Secret Name: ***Mah***
Element - Air

Yetzirah is the World of Formation. This is the realm of logic and intelligence. The intellectual world represented by the Element of Air.

Yetzirah is the world of Angelic Choirs. Here are the Seraphim and the Elohim. Choirs of Angels bring the resources that are needed to bear for completion in Assiah.

Yet they are still non-material. This is the abode of the angels, who are wrapped in luminous garments. The myriads of angels are divided into ten ranks, according to the ten sefirot, and each angel is set over a different part of the universe, and derives his name from the element or heavenly body he guards [C.D.Ginsburg, S.A.Cook, Kabbalah, p.621].

This region is interpreted in the Zohar as the world of the lower heavens, consisting of the seven plantery firmaments [Paul Krzok, "The Cosmological Structure of the Zohar", p.32 The Hermetic Journal, no.20, Summer 1983)]. The pseudo-epigraphical Massekhet Atzilut (early 14th Century), places the Archangel Metatron and the angels centered around him are placed in the world of Yetzirah rather than Beriah [Scholem, *Kabbalah*, pp.118-9].

4. ASSIAH

Olam ha-Assiah
The Material world.
The Physical world.
The Final Heh of Tettragrammaton.
Secret Name: Ben
Element - Earth.

Assiah is the world of action. this is the material world in which the results of the efforts of God become material. The Ideas that were started in Atziluth reach manifestation in Assiah.

The physical universe and Malkuth are the representation of Assiah. The four Elements are the primary building blocks and are present in the physical sense in Assiah.

This is the region of are the grossest sefirot, consisting of material substance. There are ten degrees, each lower than the other. Alternatively, there are seven earths (the highest presumably being the earth of human beings, i.e. the physical universe) one beneath the other, and beneath the lowest of them, seven hells, again arranged in sequence. In contrast to Christianity, the souls of sinners are there not only to be punished but also to be purified, before ascending, the exception being the hell of Abadon, where the soul are apparently destroyed. [Paul Krzok, "The Cosmological Structure of the Zohar", *The Hermetic Journal*, no.20, Summer 1983) pp.33-4].

The cosmos is represented in the form a tree called Treee of Life. Since Man was created as a projection of God the Tree of Life with the ten sefiroth could represent Man.

"Adam Kadmon" can be translated as "The Projection of Man." Because man is made in God's likeness, and Man is really the temple of God we should expect such a similarity in the structure and design of the temple. As such Kabbalah insists that the temple itself is in the form of man as indicated previously. The symbol of the Tree of Life is also understood to represent the spiritual projection/emanation of YHWH Elohim. This very ancient, the symbol stands at the core of Jewish mysticism. Its dynamics therefore underlie the Hebrew, the Christian, and the Muslim scriptures

Without going into details let me just graphically indicate how the Kabballistic Tree of Life with the ten sefiroth could represent Man. Those who are familiar with the Chakra of Hinduism will see the similarity here.

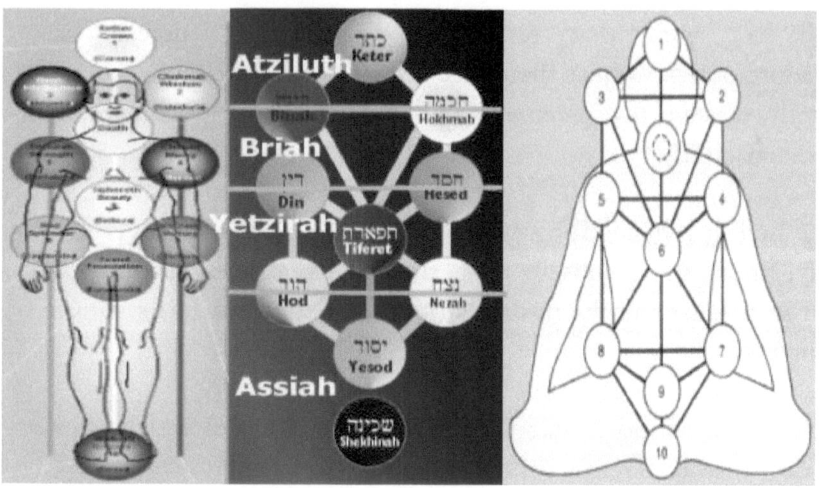

Man exists in all four dimensions

Just as the material dimensions are manifested in different forms – as the body consists of head, neck,arms, body, navel, legs connected to the mind sensation through the five senses, other dimensions are also complex with corresponding communication links to higher dimensions of existence. Thus the simplistic classification of Body, Soul and Spirit should be taken only as a broad classification.

The Kabbalistic souls

In the (13th Century) Zoharic tradition we have a sequence of increasing levels of consciousness or stages of spiritualization and transcendence in the following order: personality/physical consciousness (*nefesh*), spiritual/moral consciousness (*ruah*), and Divine consciousness (*neshamah*). In the (16th century) Lurianic tradition, we have the lower self or "animal soul" (*nefesh behemis*), then the middle self or intellect (*ruah*), and finally the higher or divine self (*neshamah*). Two higher principles were added to these three levels. In Hawaiian occultism, every person possesses three souls: a "spirit that remembers" (*unihilipi* = nefesh or subconscious), a "ghost that talks" (*uhane* = ruah or ego), and an "utterly trustworthy parental spirit" (*Aumakua* = neshamah or superconscious)

"The nefesh remains for a while in the grave, brooding over the body; the ru'ah ascends to the terrestrial paradise in accordance with its merits; and the neshamah goes directly back to its native home"

Some Kaballists postulates even seven souls, each of which after the death has different journeys and ends.

In the same way, just as the spirit of God has seven Spirits, human spirit also consists of seven spirits. Thus even though for classifications we define Mind, Body and Soul each part is more complex. This complexity extends at all levels that the whole cosmos is part of God's body. This is emphasized by Jesus in asserting that the Church is the body of Christ.

Theosis

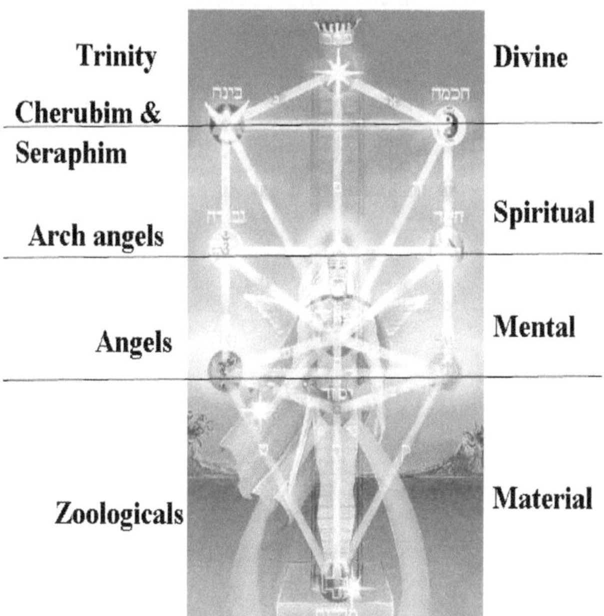

These are the four world of Hebrew Mystic cosmology. God has created conscious intelligent beings and other creations in each of these realms. In the Divine realm the first appearance of Godhead was in the form of Trinity, thus endowing himself with properties in relation to each other. The creation then procedes from there. We know that there are Cherubim and Seraphim which are close to the throne of God - the Crown. They exists in all four realms. The Arch Angels exist in the three realms below that, the Angels in the two realms below that and finally we have the zoological creatures in the material realm.

When Man was created he was created as Sons of God, a little lower than the Gods. So Man existed in the divine realm reaching down to material realm - a four dimensional existence.

Following the Kabalistic understanding of cosmos, cosmic person and of man early Christian Church interpreted the salvation as a progressive sanctification from the material level of human existence to the divine level in the Atziluth.

Psa 8:3 When I look at thy heavens, the work of thy fingers, the moon and the stars which thou hast established;

Psa 8:4 what is man that thou art mindful of him, and the son of man that thou dost care for him?

Psa 8:5 Yet thou hast made him little less than God, and dost crown him with glory and honor.

Psa 8:6 Thou hast given him dominion over the works of thy hands; thou hast put all things under his feet,

Man according to this understanding was made a divine being – a little less than God. His place is near the Kether – the Crown.

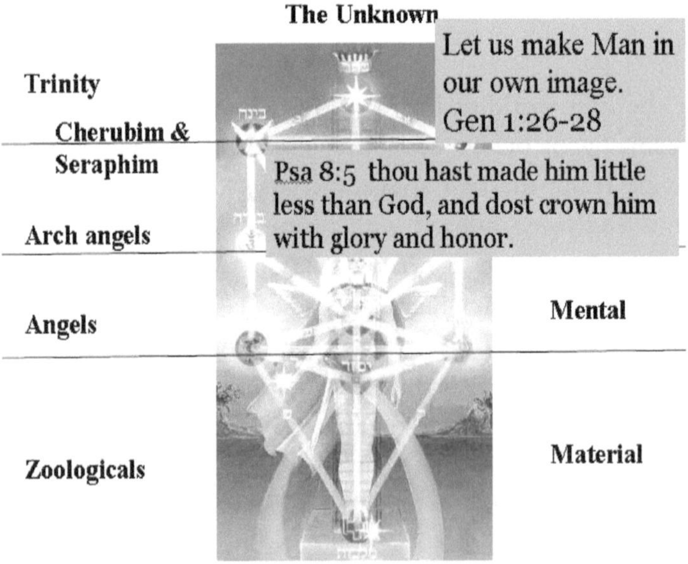

The Unknown

Let us make Man in our own image. Gen 1:26-28

Trinity

Cherubim & Seraphim

Psa 8:5 thou hast made him little less than God, and dost crown him with glory and honor.

Arch angels

Angels

Mental

Zoologicals

Material

The result of the assertion of self and seperateness resulted in the expulsion of Man from the divine realm and that dimension was closed for Mankind until the time of redemption

However due to the fall Man lost than level and caused himself to be creatures of material realm (Assiah) like the animals and the plants. Hence he is kept under the authority and supervision of Angels that exists in the spiritual and mental realm (Briah and Yetzira) until he is redeemed. Salvation is this process of redemption. In order to achieve this Jesus himself enters into Assiah

Heb 2:5 For it was not to angels that God subjected the world to come, of which we are speaking.

Heb 2:6 It has been testified somewhere, "What is man that thou art mindful of him, or the son of man, that thou carest for him?

Heb 2:7 Thou didst make him for a little while lower than the angels, thou hast crowned him with glory and honor,

Heb 2:8 putting everything in subjection under his feet." Now in putting everything in subjection to him, he left nothing outside his control. As it is, we do not yet see everything in subjection to him.

Heb 2:9 But we see Jesus, who for a little while was made lower than the angels, crowned with glory and honor because of the suffering of death, so that by the grace of God he might taste death for every one.

Heb 2:10 For it was fitting that he, for whom and by whom all things exist, in bringing many sons to glory, should make the pioneer of their salvation perfect through suffering.

Heb 2:11 For he who sanctifies and those who are sanctified have all one origin. That is why he is not ashamed to call them brethren,

In the above passage the author of Hebrew quotes Psalms but refers "lower than angels" instead of "lower than God" thereby indicating the present status of man below that of angels. But verse 11 asserts that man is of the same origin as Jesus – Both emanating from God. While Jesus is called the Only begotten Son (monogenes) of the Father, Adam is called son (huios) of God.

Luk 3:38 (the ***son)*** *of Enos, (the* ***son)*** *of Seth, (the* ***son)*** *of* ***Adam****, (the* ***son)*** *of* ***God.***

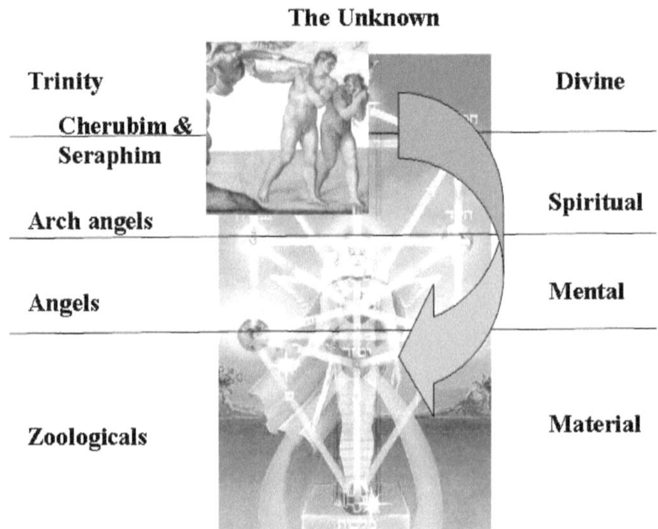

Thus though originally Man was supposed to be one of the Sons of God he was put under the tutelage of the Angels for a little while. These Sons who are in the infant stage were to learn obedience and suffering. Thus Man came to be little lower than the Angels for a while.

Gal 3:23 Now before faith came, we were confined under the law, kept under restraint until faith should be revealed.

Mankind will be redeemed and given the status of the Children of God through the redemption that comes from Jesus.

Joh 1:14 And the Word became flesh and dwelt among us, full of grace and truth; we have beheld his glory, glory as of the only Son from the Father.

Joh 1:18 No one has ever seen God; the only Son, who is in the bosom of the Father, he has made him known.

Joh 3:16 For God so loved the world that he gave his only Son, that whoever believes in him should not perish but have eternal life.
Joh 3:17 For God sent the Son into the world, not to condemn the world, but that the world might be saved through him.

There is a difference in category but they are both of the same origin. It is in this context that the Eastern Churches talk about the process of progressive sanctification as theosis or deification.

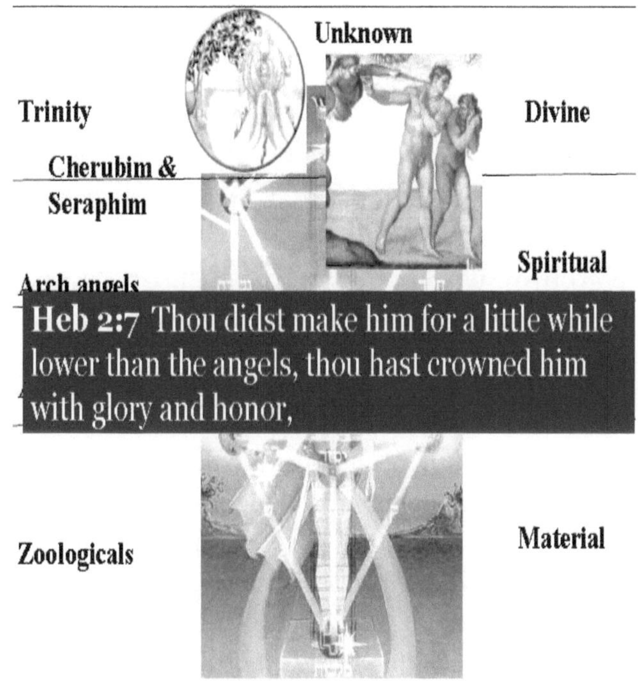

Rom 8:14-17 For all who are led by the Spirit of God are sons of God. For you did not receive the spirit of slavery to fall back into fear, but you have received the spirit of sonship.
When we cry, "Abba! Father!" it is the Spirit himself bearing witness with our spirit that we are children of God, and if children, then heirs, heirs of God and fellow heirs

with Christ, provided we suffer with him in order that we may also be glorified with him.

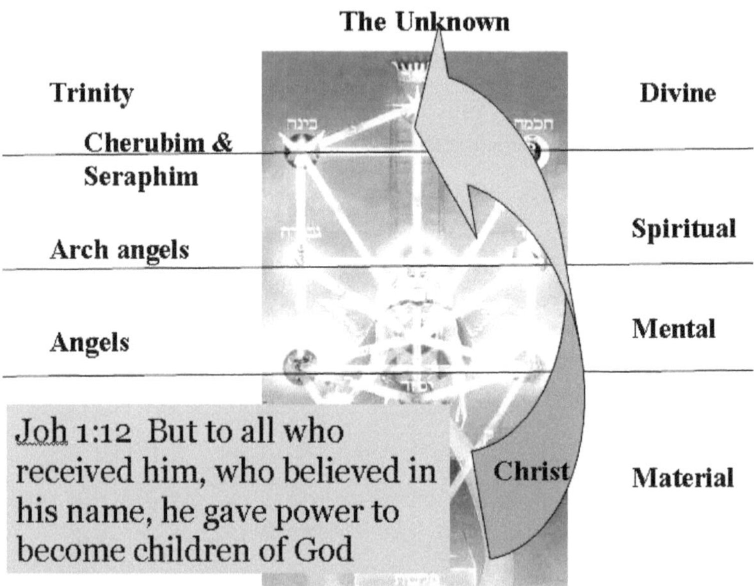

Deification is the process of becoming "as much as possible like and in union with God" -- a "participation through grace in that which surrounds the nature of God." It was realized perfectly and fully in the Incarnation of the Son of God, in Whom "generic" human nature was deified. This nature of man had been established in the Creation for communion with God, but it was "darkened by its existential condition subsequent to Adam's sin." Deification is the restoration of the intended communion between God and man, beginning with the human life and death of Christ. Thus, Deification describes the Eastern understanding of *salvation in Christ.* It lies behind the Christology of Athanasius, the Cappadocian Fathers, Cyril of Alexandria, John of Damascus, *etc.* "God became man, that man might become divine."

At the Council of Nicaea, the confession of the Son as *homoousios* (one in essence) with the Father declares that fellowship with Christ must be understood as communion with God, *i.e.*, as Deification.

Likewise, at the Council of Constantinople, the confession of the Holy Spirit as divine was also required, since "deification of man as sanctification is rooted in the work of the Holy Spirit." If the Spirit was not true God, then "man would be neither sanctified nor deified." "(Theosis," *The Oxford Dictionary of Byzantium*, edited by Alexander P. Kazhdan, *et al.* (1991): 2069)

2 Corinthians 3:18 But we all, with open face beholding as in a glass the glory of the Lord, are changed into the same image from glory to glory, *even* as by the Spirit of the Lord.

The Greek word for "changed" is "metamorphoo" which is a transfiguring, a change such as Jesus underwent on the Mount of Transfiguration. The "Doxa Kuriou" the Glory of the Lord is what man is changed into, following Paul's understanding wherein he notes "auton eikona metamorphoumetha" which is changed from glory to glory into the same image

Deification means we are to become more like God through His grace or divine energies. In creation, humans were made in the image and likeness of God (Gen.1:26) according to human nature. In other words, humanity by nature is an icon or image of deity: The divine image is in all humanity. Through sin, however, this image and likeness of God was marred, and we fell.

When the Son of God assumed our humanity in the womb of the blessed Virgin Mary, the process of our being renewed in God's image and likeness was begun. Thus, those who are joined to Christ through faith in Holy Baptism begin a re-creation process, being renewed in God's image and likeness. We become, as St Peter writes, 'partakers of the divine nature" (2 Pet. 1:4).

Because of the Incarnation of the Son of God, because the fullness of God has inhabited human flesh, being joined to Christ means that it is again possible to experience deification, the fulfillment of our human destiny. That is, through union with Christ, we become by grace what God is by nature-we 'become children of God' (John 1:12). His deity interpenetrates our humanity.

And I have given them the glory you gave me, so that they may be one, as we are one, I in them and you in me, that they may be brought to perfection as one, that the world may know that you sent me, and that you loved them even as you loved me. (Jesus--John 17:22-23, New American Bible)

For those who are led by the Spirit of God are children of God. For you did not receive a spirit of slavery to fall back into fear, but you received a spirit of adoption, through which we cry, "Abba, Father!" The Spirit itself bears witness with our spirit that we are children of God, and if children, then heirs, heirs of God and joint heirs with Christ, if only we suffer with him so that we may also be glorified with him. (St. Paul--Romans 8:14-17, New American Bible)

His divine power has bestowed on us everything that makes for life and devotion, through the knowledge of him who called us by his own glory and power. Through these, he has bestowed on us the precious and very great promises, so that through them you may come to share in the divine nature, after escaping from the corruption that is in the world because of evil desire. (St. Peter--2 Peter 1:3-4, New American Bible)

He was made a sharer in our mortality. He made us sharers in His deity. (St. Augustine)

Man's life is a strenuous and endless ascent toward God, that is, deification. (St. Gregory of Nyssa, taken from Achieving Your Potential in Christ: Theosis by Anthony Coniaris)

We have become like Christ, for Christ became like us. We have become gods through Him, for He became man for us. (St. Gregory Nazianzen, Achieving Your Potential in Christ: Theosis by Anthony Coniaris)

We know our God from His energies, but we do not claim that we can draw near to His essence, for His energies come down to us, but His essence remains unapproachable. (St. Basil the Great, Achieving Your Potential in Christ: Theosis by Anthony Coniaris)

Athanasius
"God became man so that men might become gods." "The Word was made flesh in order that we might be enabled to be made gods .... Just as the Lord, putting on the body, became a man, so also we men are both deified through his flesh, and henceforth inherit everlasting life "

Ephraim the syrian
"He gave us divinity. We gave him humanity."

Augustine
"But he himself that justifies also deifies, for by justifying he makes sons of God. 'For he has given them power to become the sons of God' [John 1: 12]. If then we have been made sons of God, we have also been made gods

C. S. Lewis,
"The command Be ye perfect is not idealistic gas. Nor is it a command to do the impossible. He is going to make us into creatures that can obey that command. He said (in the Bible) that

we were "gods" and He is going to make good His words. If we let Him--for we can prevent Him, if we choose --He will make the feeblest and filthiest of us into a god or goddess, dazzling, radiant, immortal creature, pulsating all through with such energy and joy and wisdom and love as we cannot now imagine, a bright stainless mirror which reflects back to God perfectly (though, of course, on a smaller scale) His own boundless power and delight and goodness. The process will be long and in parts very painful; but that is what we are in for. Nothing less. He meant what He said. "

Rom 6:5 For if **we** *have been united with* **him** *in a death* **like** *his,* **we shall** *certainly be united with* **him** *in a resurrection* **like** *his.*
1Jo 3:2 Beloved, **we** *are God's children now; it does not yet appear what* **we shall** *be, but* **we** *know that when he appears* **we shall** *be* **like him***, for* **we shall** *see* **him** *as he is.*

The picture of the saints forming the body of Christ and the Church as an organism forming the bride of Christ who will ultimately united with Christ is the picture given here. So our relationship with God as New Man is like the relationship between the husband and wife. United, made whole, but distinct in personality.

Mat 19:5 and said, 'For this reason a man shall **leave** *his* **father** *and mother and be joined to his wife, and the two shall become* **one flesh***'?*

Co 11:2 I feel a divine jealousy for you, for I betrothed you to Christ to present you as a pure bride to her one husband.
Rev 19:7 Let us rejoice and exult and give him the glory, for the marriage of the Lamb has come, and his **Bride** *has made herself ready;*

Mat 19:5 and said, 'For this reason a man shall **leave** *his* **father** *and mother and be joined to his wife, and the two shall become* **one flesh***'?*

APPENDIX 1

HNDU: PANCHA- KOSAS AND SAPTHA CHAKRAS

As described in Dvidiya Prasna of Taitriya Upanishad: Ananda Valli or Brahma Valli
http://www.vedarahasya.net/ananda.htm

It will be interesting to compare other models with the Biblical Model. The Hindu model is a five dimensional model. There are three sheaths for man subdivisible as five. These are:

Sthula Sareera :Gross Body: made up of gross matter

1. Food sheath (Anna-maya kosa)
   The five organs of perception
   and the five organs of action are a part of it. It is called food sheath because it is caused by food, maintained by food; and finally ends up as food

2. Vital-Air sheath (Prana-maya kosa)
   There are five faculties of man. They correspond to the five physiological functions. They are called the five

Pranas dependent on air. These are:
Prana :Perception (five senses) – seeing, hearing, smelling, tasting, touching
Apana : excretion- faeces, urine, sperms, sputum, perspiration
Samana: digestion
Vyana: circulation
Udana: thought

Sukshma Sareera : Subtle Body : constituting of passions, desires, emotions, feelings and thoughts.

3. Mental sheath (Mana-maya kosa) – Those faculties connected with the mind. These are: passions and emotions, feelings and impulses.

4. Intellectual sheath (Vignana-maya kosa): These are: thinking, reasoning, discriminating, judging etc.

Karana Sareera : Causal Body: storehouse of all impressions and latent energies

5. Bliss sheath (Ananda-maya kosa) Vasanas as experienced in sleep state. There are various levels in this as seen through the deep sleep state, dreaming state, waking state.

One should go beyond all the five sheaths in order to experience bliss. This state is known as Turiya or Mahakaarana Swarupa (supreme causal aspect). This comes after Sushupti (deep sleep state). This is also referred to as Paaramaarthika. The bliss experienced in the state of Turiya is the true bliss

There are five types of Kleshas (obstacles), which come in the way of experiencing this bliss. They are :
Avidya Klesha, obstacles due to ignorance
Abinava Klesha, obstacles because one do not exercise control over the mind and are carried away by vain imaginations.
Asthitha Klesha, arises out of interest in worldly pleasures
Raaga Klesha, results from attachment towards wealth and material objects
and
Dwesha Klesha. arises when one's desires are not fulfilled.

This is very much parallel to the following quote from http://www.rezlife.net/tripartite.html

"Our five sense are like five kings. When we are not being led by the Spirit of God, we are being led by: sight, sound, smell, touch, and taste. All of these natural senses have spiritual operations. In Joshua , Joshua put five kings in a cave and covered them up by a rock.

The five kings cause these things to be prominent in our lives: (1) self-elevation (2) self-exaltation (3) self-establishment (4) self-motivation (5) self-worship.

- Self-elevation is idol worship because we want to ascend unto the heavens in order to be noticed.
- When we exalt ourselves, we take glory from man's approval. We want man's approval more than God's approval, thus causing us to fear man instead of having the fear of the Lord.
- Self-establishment causes us to want a kingdom to rule over. This king is found in churches when they strive to establish their ministry instead of the ministry of God. This causes churches to

only want to feed themselves spiritually instead of reaching out to others.

- If you are self-motivated, you live a life filled with lust, pride, self-will, and self-pity.
- Self-worship is the love of self which causes us to think that the world revolves around us.

These kings have to be put under the Rock of Jesus. They have to be conquered by the Sword of the Spirit.

How do we come to a place where we can submit our soul to the Spirit of God? In order to do this we must let the Sword of the Spirit cut away the carnal desires that are in our heart. What is the Sword of the Spirit? The answer to this question is found in Ephesians 6:17.

Ephesians 6:17 And take the helmet of salvation, and the sword of the Spirit, which is the word of God.

We must allow the word of God to cut away our carnal mind which is enmity to God.

In Hebrews 4:12, the scripture tells us that the word of God will divide asunder the soul and spirit, and will separate the thoughts and intents of the heart. The word of God reveals to us what is in our heart and shows us what is the heart of God. We have to let the operation of the Sword of the Spirit cut away the thoughts and intents of our own heart that are not of God.

Hebrews 4:12 For the word of God is quick, and powerful, and sharper than any two-edged sword, piercing even to the dividing asunder of soul and spirit, and of the joints and marrow, and is a discerner of the thoughts and intents of the heart.

A similar five sheath structure is developed by James A. Fowler in Constitution of Man (http://www.christinyou.net/pages/constman.html) where he uses the following diagram.

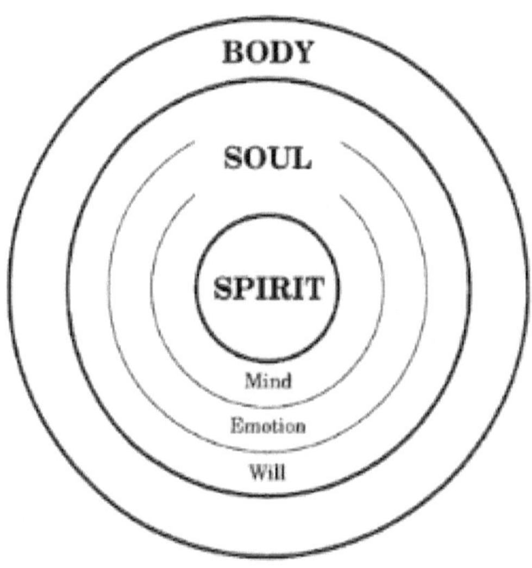

There are others who divide the Kosas into seven part corresponding to the seven charkas. Each of these Kosas extends from the body beyond the physical and merges with the universe. The concept behind is that man is not a being who is separated from the rest of the world. He is very much part and parcel of the universe and universal consciousness and exists in a multidimensional world of consciousness dimension. The person who realizes the various levels of chakra is able to experience and sense these higher dimensions of his existence. The highest of this is realized when Man enjoins the fullest oneness with the ultimate.

The Seven Kosas (Body Sheaths or Aura) and Corresponding States of Consciousness:

The chakras and Kundalini came to be an integral part of yoga philosophy in the non-dual Tantric tradition, which arose in the 7th century.

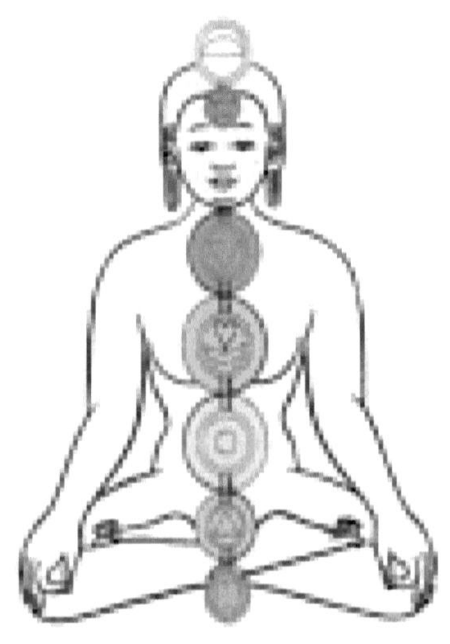

	Sanskrit Name	**Location**	**Consciousness**	**Kosa**	**Dimension**
Root (1)	Muladhara (root/support)	Base of spine	emerging consciousness (vyutthana citta)	Annamaya body boundary	Physical
Sacral (2)	Svadhisthana (sweetness)	Abdomen, Genitals, lower back, hips	restraining consciousness (nirodha citta)	Pranamaya 1-3 inches extension beyond body	Emotional Indriya Sense based
Solar Plexus (3)	Manipura (lustrous Jewl)	Solar Plexus	individualized consciousness (nirmana citta)	Mental body (manomaya kosa) 3-8 inches around	Ego

				the physical body	
Heart (4)	Anahata (unstruck)	Heart "area"	tranquil consciousness (prasanta citta)	intellectual body (vijnanamaya kosa) 6-12 inches around the physical body	Astral
Throat (5)	Visshudha (purification)	Throat	attentive consciousness (ekagrata citta)	the body of joy (anandamaya kosa) 12-24 inches around the physical body	Creative
Brow (6)	Ajna (to perceive)	Brow	fissured or rent consciousness (chidra citta)	the body of consciousness (cittamaya kosa) 24-30 inches around the physical body	Celestial Archetypal
Crown (7)	Sahasrara (thousandfold)	Top of head, cerebral cortex	pure consciousness (paripakva citta or divya citta)	the body of the self (atmamaya kosa) beyond 30 inches of body into cosmos	Universal

APPENDIX II

JIVA-TATTVA OF JAIN RELIGION

Cosmos consists of two types of dravyas (elements or entities) Jiva (sentient beings) and Ajiva (non sentient things). Jainism attributes life to all bodies. The Ajiva are basic constituents from which the bodies are made. They are permanent, eternal, uncreated and of immense magnitude. They undergo changes (Paryaya) but retains their maintain their Guna (properties).

AJIVA : The Non Sentient entities are:

(1) Dharmastikay (Medium of Motion).
(2) Adharmastikay (Medium of Rest).
(3) Akashastikay (Space).
(4) Pudgalastikay (Matter).
(5) Kal (Time).

JIVA

Jiva is the result of joining of **Soul and Body**. Jivas are defined as that which grows, decays, fluctuates, varies, eats, sleeps, awakes, acts, fears, rests, has knowledge and perception, attempts to self defend, and reproduces. When the soul leaves a body these qualities cease. This also makes it clear that the body and the soul are separate entities.

Jivas are categorized in two groups.

1. **Siddha** or Liberated Jiva

Liberated souls have no karmas and therefore, they are no longer in the cycle of birth and death. They do not live among us, but reside at the uppermost part of this universe called Siddhashila. They are formless and shapeless, have perfect knowledge and perception, and have infinite vigor and bliss. All siddhas are equal and there is no difference in their status. These are beings who once walked in human form and attained the liberation from birth and death.

2. **Sansari Jiva** or Non-liberated Jiva

.

On the other side, non-liberated jivas have karmas, and are continually going through the cycle of birth and death. They experience happiness and pain and have passions. They have limited knowledge and perception.

Senses and Living beings

There are five senses - touch, taste, smell, sight and hearing. There is a gradation in the Jiva based on the number of senses they posses. They are also categorized in terms of their mobility – Sthävar Jiva those that do not move and have only one sense and Trasa jiva those that move which may have two or more senses.

Ekendriya Jiva (with only one sense organ)

Ekendriya Jiva (One sense organ beings) are non mobile and has only one sense. They are further classified into five groups:

(1) those that have **Prithwikäya** or earth based bodies like clay, sand, metal, and coral, etc.
(2) those that have **Apkäya** or water based bodied like dew, fog, iceberg, and rain, etc. .
(3) those that have **Väyukäya** or air based bodies like wind, storms, whirlwinds, and cyclones, etc.
(4) those that have **Teukäya** or fire based bodies like flames, blaze, lightening, forest fire, and hot ash, etc.
(5) those that have **Vanaspatikäya** or plant bodies.

> There are two types of Plants: Plants like Trees, plants, bushes, stem,branches, leaves, and seeds, etc has only one soul in one body and are called **Pratyek Vanaspatikäya**.
> Plants that can continue to live life after life are given multiple souls. These are called **Sädhäran Vanaspatikäya**. Examples are Roots such as potatoes, carrots, onions, garlic, beats, etc. belong to this category. Some of these are even considered to have an infinite number of souls and are called **anantakaya**.

Tras Jiva, Bahu Indriya Jiva
(those with more than one sense organ)

The Mobile multiple sensed beings (Tras jiva, multi sensed being, bahu indriya jiva) are divided according to the number of senses they have

(1) **Beindriya Jiva** :Those with two senses: touch, and taste: e.g. shells, worms, insects, microbes, termites, etc.

(2) **Treindriya Jiva:** Those with three senses: touch, taste, and smell; e.g. bugs, lice, white ants, moths, centipedes, etc.

(3) **Chaurindriya Jiva** : Those with four senses: touch, taste, smell and sight
e.g. scorpions, crickets, spiders, beetles, locusts, flies, etc.

(4) **Panchendriya Jiva**: Those with five senses: touch, taste, smell, sight and hearing
e.g. human beings, animals, fish, birds, etc.

<u>Ten Prans</u>

Depending upon the development of the Jiva, there are up to ten kinds of prans or vitalities present in each jiva. These vitalities are:

1) Sparsh-Indriya (Touch): The ability to feel the sensation of touch
2) Ras-Indriya (Taste): the ability to taste
3) Ghran-Indriya (Smell): the ability to smell
4) Chakshu-Indriya (Vision): the ability to see
5) Shravan-Indriya (Hearing): the ability to hear
6) Mano-bal (Mind): the ability to think
7) Vachan-bal (Speech): the ability to speak
8) Kaya-bal (Body): the ability to move the body
9) Shwasochchhwas (Respiration): the ability to inhale and exhale
10) Ayushya (Longevity): the ability to live

The Ekendriya jivas possess only the first four prans
The beindriya jivas possess the first six prans
The treindriya jivas possess the first seven prans

The chaurindriya jivas possess the first eight prans
The panchendriya jivas are divided into two groups:
(1) The **asangni (non-sentient) jivas**, whose minds are not developed and
(2) The **sangni (sentient) jivas**, whose minds are fully developed.

The asangni panchendriya jivas possess nine prans
The sangni panchendriya jivas possess all ten pranas.

Sentient Jivas and Moksha Prapti

This class is divided into four classes
a) **Näraki**: Jivas living in hell,
b) **Tiryancha** - Non-human beings like animals, birds, fish,etc.
c) **Manushya** - Human beings.
d) **Deva** - heavenly beings,

These four classes in their order are of increasing state of happiness. Those that live in hell are in total suffering to those that live in heaven are in highest happiness. Both ends of the spectrum of beings suffer because they hinder them from using their mind either because of pain or pleasure. They can never attain Moksha because of that. The human existence is the most preferable because during this life one can use logic to the fullest extent, can perform austerities, can live with restraint, and thus can attain Moksha. Hence the lucky lives are those who are born as human because this is the only chance one gets to attain Salvation.

APPENDIX III

BUDDHISM AND NO-SOUL

Unlike Jainism Buddhism negates the existence of a separate entity called soul. Buddhism denies the existence of an unchanging or eternal soul created by a God or emanating from a Divine Essence *(Paramatma)*. They consider consciousness as an ever changing mental state based on the sensations of mind like heat or cold, light or shade, love or hatred, pain or pleasure. But these are not permanent.

What appears to be an individual person is actually a changing process of mental and physical qualities combining temporarily in a particular way. Through possessive attachment, the mind identifies with part or all of this process, and this gives rise to the thought of 'me' and 'mine'. In fact, all phenomena, animate or inanimate, are dependently arisen from causes and conditions.

This is summarily presented by Venerable Narada Thera, in Buddhism in a Nutshell
http://www.buddhanet.net/e-learning/buddhism/nshell09.htm as follows:

"According to Buddhism mind is nothing but a complex compound of fleeting mental states. One unit of consciousness consists of three phases

— arising or genesis (*uppada*) static or development (*thiti*), and cessation or dissolution (*bhanga*). Immediately after the cessation stage of a thought moment there occurs the genesis stage of the subsequent thought-moment. Each momentary consciousness of this ever-changing life-process, on passing away, transmits its whole energy, all the indelibly recorded impressions to its successor. Every fresh consciousness consists of the potentialities of its predecessors together with something more. There is therefore, a continuous flow of consciousness like a stream without any interruption. The subsequent thought moment is neither absolutely the same as its predecessor — since that which goes to make it up is not identical — nor entirely another — being the same continuity of kamma energy. Here there is no identical being but there is an identity in process. ….

If there is no soul, what is it that is reborn, one might ask. Well, there is nothing to be reborn.

When life ceases the kammic energy re-materializes itself in another form. … When one mode of its manifestation ceases it merely passes on, and where suitable circumstances offer, reveals itself afresh in another name or form."

APPENDIX IV

ANIMAL SOUL

The question whether animals have soul had been a hotly debated question since immemorial times. This is important because it brings us to the problem of freewill and responsibility. The Greek Philosopher Aristotle (384 –322 BC)
(http://classics.mit.edu/Aristotle/soul.html) postulated a gradations of faculties from inanimate matter to man. Matter is inanimate. Plants on the other hand has functions of nourishment and reproduction. Animals, have more degree of freedom - sensation, motion, and all degrees of mental functions except reason. Finally logic and reason were the uniqueness of man. His threefold classification of souls runs thus:

Nutritive souls have the capacity for procreation and absorbing nutrition (plants). Animate souls have the capacity for desire, locomotion, sensation, and imagination (animals). Intellective souls have the capacity for mathematical reasoning and philosophy (humans). A human is a rational (differentia) animal (genus). An animal is an animate living thing. A living thing is a nutritive soul imposed on some mixture of elements. The elements are different combinations of hot, cold, wet, and dry in prime matter

St. Thomas Aquinas (1225–1274 AD) (http://members.aol.com/wheregod/chapters/aquin07d.htm) in *Summa contra Gentiles*, following Aristotle, held that animals were "moved by nature" and not "by art." Lacking both understanding and reason, the animal soul was rooted in the physical body in a way the human soul was not. "Therefore [the animal soul] perishes when the body perishes,"

Rene Descartes (1596 – 1650 AD)
(http://www.vegans.org.uk/descartes.html)
(http://www.newadvent.org/cathen/04744b.htm) who lived at the turn of the modern science considered that animals are pure machines, while men are machines with minds. Rapid increase in experimental sciences of physics and biology supported the mechanistic view of nature. Descartes argued that animal motions like physiological functions (such as digestion), reactions; (such as blinking, and feelings (such as passions)do not depend on the mind. They are simply biological processes. In man, however, the mind could also direct the course of the fluid ("animal spirits") which controls movements. "It thus appears that there is but one type of organization in the universe, and that man is the most perfect example" (La Mettrie's "L'Homme machine ." *Man a Machine*, translated by Gertrude Bussey, La Salle, Ill., 1953, p. 140; cf. Vartanian ed., p. 190).

Leibniz (1646–1716)
(http://www.rbjones.com/rbjpub/philos/classics/leibniz/monad.htm) postulated the principle of continuity in beings. The matter, plants, animals and man are different in their order of sensitivity. 'If we are willing to give the name 'soul' to everything which has perceptions and appetites (in the general sense I have just explained), then all created simple substances (monads) could be called 'souls'. But since sensation is something more than simple perception, I am prepared to accept that the general name 'monad' or 'entelechy' is sufficient for simple substances which only have simple perceptions, and that we should reserve the name

'soul' for those which have more distinct perceptions accompanied by memory." "Nature has given heightened perceptions to animals, through the care it has taken to supply them with sense organs, which bring together many rays of light or waves in the air, to make them more effective by being united. There is something similar in the senses of smell, taste, and touch, and perhaps also many other senses which are unknown to us." "But it is knowledge of necessary and eternal truths which distinguishes us from mere animals, and which gives us *reason* and the sciences, by elevating us to knowledge of ourselves and of God. This is what in us is called the 'rational soul', or *spirit*."

Rudolf Steiner (1861-1925) distinguishes body, mind and soul into several levels (http://www.kheper.net/topics/Anthroposophy/Steiner-levels_of_self.htm)

<table>
<tr><td>3-fold</td><td>9-fold</td><td>7-fold</td><td>4-fold</td></tr>
<tr><td rowspan="3">SPIRIT</td><td>Spirit Man</td><td>Atma</td><td rowspan="3">future stages / angelic consciousness</td></tr>
<tr><td>Life Spirit</td><td>Buddhi</td></tr>
<tr><td>Spirit Self</td><td>Manas</td></tr>
<tr><td rowspan="3">SOUL</td><td>Spiritual Soul</td><td rowspan="2">Ego</td><td rowspan="2">Ego</td></tr>
<tr><td>Intellectual Soul</td></tr>
<tr><td>Sentient Soul</td><td rowspan="2">Astral body</td><td rowspan="2">Astral body</td></tr>
<tr><td>BODY</td><td>Soul Body</td></tr>
</table>

	Etheric Body	Etheric Body	Etheric Body
	Physical body	Physical body	Physical body

He divides the cosmos into four kingdoms:

Physical	**Etheric** **Physical**	**Astral** **Etheric** **Physicsal**	**Ego** **Astral** **Etheric** **Physical**
mineral	Plant	Animal	Man

Teilhard de Chardin, Pierre (1881–1955) Geologist, palaeontologist, Jesuit priest, and philosopher, in his major work, *Le Phénomène humain* (written 1938–40, The Phenomenon of Humanity argues that humanity is in a continuous process of evolution towards a perfect spiritual state. .

Teilhard's says "We are faced with a harmonized collectivity of consciousnesses to a sort of superconciousness. The earth not only becoming covered by myriads of grains of thought, but becoming enclosed in a single thinking envelope, a single unanimous reflection." (1961, pp. 251-2) Yet such a unanimity of consciousness implies a condition that humans generally reject, depersonalization. Indeed, the conclusion seems inevitable: "So that at the world's Omega, as at its

Alpha, lies the Impersonal." (p. 258) At this point, "Omega," the last letter in the Greek alphabet, simply refers to the final stage of evolution. At the end the noosphere become an "all" that absorbs all. It has been uphill task till now. At this point we have a choice either to move towards the omega point through love or to dissipate and scatter through hate.

http://perso.wanadoo.fr/jacques.abbatucci/thephenomenon.htm

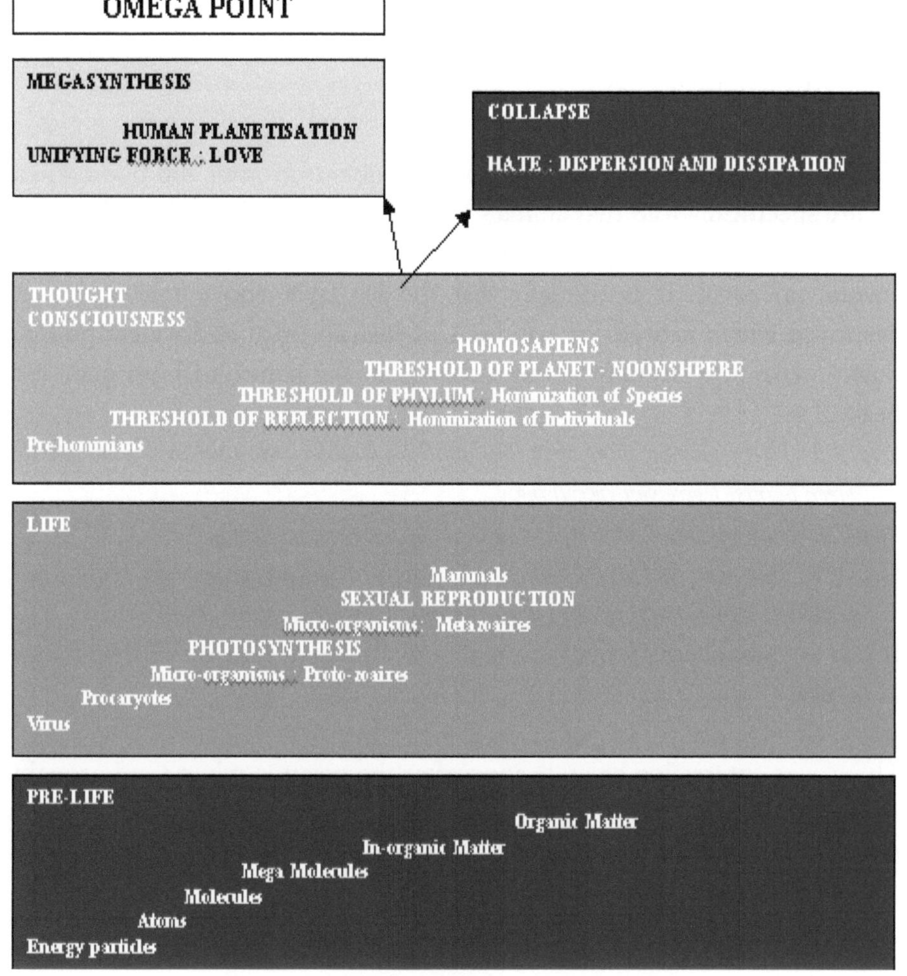

WHAT DOES THE BIBLE SAY

Having given the philosophical development of the concept of soul and the dabate on the soul of animals we will now look into the bible to see what it says about the soul. Bible do not directly address this problem. In the early Christian era, the superiority of man was stressed and most churches began to justify the sacrifice and butchering of animals by asserting that animals do not have a soul. However in the Jewish thought sacrifice of animals will be valid only on the basis of substitution – animal sacrificed in place of the self. In that case the soul of animal is an essential part of the principle of sacrifice.

Killing of animals were sanctioned in the bible only after the flood when we are specifically told that animals became wild. We know that the post-flood life expectations came down rapidly as a result of some form of cosmic upheaval (It is thought that the ice layer above the earth was destroyed which caused the windows of heaven open and waters poured down) This also brought about a change in the nature of both man and beast.

Gen 9:3 Every moving thing that lives shall be food for you; and as I gave you the green plants, I give you everything.

Gen 9:4 Only you shall not eat flesh with its life, that is, its blood.

Gen 9:5 For your lifeblood I will surely require a reckoning; of every beast I will require it and of man; of every man's brother I will require the life of man.

It was an equal bargain between man and animal as a result of the change in nature.

There is an interesting episode soon after the creation when God brought animals to Adam.

Gen 2:18 Then the LORD God said, "It is not good that the man should be alone; I will make him a helper fit for him."

Gen 2:19 So out of the ground the LORD God formed every beast of the field and every bird of the air, and brought them to the man to see what he would call them; and whatever the man called every living creature, that was its name.

Gen 2:20 The man gave names to all cattle, and to the birds of the air, and to every beast of the field; but for the man there was not found a helper fit for him.

The purpose of bringing the animals was with the intent of fellowship and friendship. How could man find a soul mate among the animals if they did not have a soul.

The alternative was to make woman. Woman was the best and fitting alternative because both man and woman exist in the same dimensions and could fellowship best. Thus we may conclude that there is an indication regarding the nature of the animal soul in that story.

It will be foolish of us to expect to understand animals and birds and ants and fishes because we have no understanding of their realm of existence. Do they talk Philosophy? Do they know about God? We simply cannot make a judgment on them because of our ignorance. They may be having an existence in dimensions where we have no share and we will never be able to understand them fully.

However Bible clearly refers to varying levels of creation – levels of life.

1Co 15:38 But God gives it a body as he has chosen, and to each kind of seed its own body.

1Co 15:39 For not all flesh is alike, but there is one kind for men, another for animals, another for birds, and another for fish.

1Co 15:40 There are celestial bodies and there are terrestrial bodies; but the glory of the celestial is one, and the glory of the terrestrial is another.

1Co 15:41 There is one glory of the sun, and another glory of the moon, and another glory of the stars; for star differs from star in glory.

It is evident that Paul is thinking in terms of the Jewish mystic teachings of existence of beings. We have seen in Kabbala that cosmos is four dimensional leaving out the dark unknown God's realm. These are indeed Material, Mind, Spirit, and Divine. Not only that there are beings which are in each of these realm, there are beings that share the dimensions in varying order. It is certainly taught that the redeemed Man is expected to be in all four dimensions – created little lower than the gods. Thus there is nothing in the Bible which will forbid animals with some extension within these realms. The difference is only in terms of degrees.

APPENDIX V

The Ancient Egyptian Concept of Man

To the Ancient Egyptians, apart from the physical form, but there were eight immortal or semi-divine parts. These are:

- **Xat (Khat)** - The Physical Body. The mummy in the tomb, thought to house the ba after death, Represented as a fish.

My Khat is buried

. Book of the Dead, Chapter LXXXVI., l. 11.

- **Ka** - The double of man inhabiting the body and remain to exist even after death and is represented as a a pair of upraised arms. The Ka has the following powers: Can wander about at will. Is independent of the man and can dwell in any statue etc of him. Can eat and drink.

-  **Ba** - "Animation" or "manifestation," which correspond closely to the modern concept of "soul." It was depicted as a human-headed bird. Ba seems to be able to assume a material or immaterial form at will.
- **Swt or Khaibit** - the unconscious. The shadow of a man associated with the physical body but capable of independent existence for a time. References to the Khaibit are infrequent, and its meaning obscure. It is represented by a fan; an object which intercepts the light
-  **Ax (Akhu, Akh, Khu, Ikhu)** - the divine intelligence. The "Transfigured spirit" into which the dead were transformed after the funerary rituals were completed It ascendes to the heavens to live with the gods.This is represented by the ibis or phoenix. As spirit, the akh is the opposite of the perishable body, kha. "Akh is for heaven, kha is for earth"
-  **Sahu** - The incorruptible spiritual body of man Sahu forms the habitation of the soul; springs from the material body. Within it, all the mental and spiritual attributes of the natural body are united to its powers. A body which has obtained a degree of knowledge and power and has thus become incorruptible; it associates with the soul, and can ascend into heaven and dwell with the gods.
-  **Sekhem** -The power or form. The incorporeal personification of the vital force of a man, dwelling in heaven among the *Khu*s.
-  **Ab (Ib)** - The heart, this was the source of good and evil within a person. At the end of life this is weighed against the feather on the head of the judge Maat. If the weight is less it will be eaten by Maat and is given eternal life if it weighs equal. with the gods after death, or be eaten by Ammut as the final death if it

failed to weigh equally against This is represented as a vessel with ears as handles

- ***Rn*** - The name was regarded as an essential part of an individual, as necessary for the survival of the deceased in the After-life as the ba, akh, and the preserved corpse. The name of an individual was preserved by its inclusion in funerary texts, either on papyrus or on the tomb walls. Should they wish to do so, later generations could destroy the existence and memory of a deceased individual by removing their name from their tomb.

2\. *mu - k* *er* *pet* *χa - k* *er* *ta*

Thy essence is in heaven, thy body to earth.[1] (VIth dynasty.)

3\. *pet* *χer* *ba - k* *ta* *χeri* *tut - k*

Heaven hath thy soul, earth hath thy body.[2] (Ptolemaïc period.)

While it is difficult to understand the complicated and subtle differences in the Egyptian concept of man, it is certainly based on the idea that a man has several dimensions of existence with several types of bodies and several corresponding souls. These is a physical body which returns to earth and the physical soul cease to exist. There is a planetary body which survive the death and continues to live at least for a time. Then there is the astral body and the cosmic body. These continue long after the normal death. The cosmic body is immortal.

Caroline Seawright
http://www.touregypt.net/magazine/mag05012001/magf3.htm

ORIENTAL INSTITUTE RESEARCH ARCHIVES
http://www-oi.uchicago.edu/OI/DEPT/RA/Research_Arch.html
http://www.kheper.net/topics/Egypt/egyptian_soul.htm

http://www.advancedresearchconsultants.com/ancient_egypt.htm

Ancient Egyptian Mythology: A Model for Consciousness
http://www.janetcunningham.com/article_egypt.html

42 Negative Confessions. Against which the heart is judged .

1. ***I have not done iniquity.***
2. ***I have not robbed with violence.***
3. ***I have not stolen.***
4. ***I have done no murder; I have done no harm.***
5. ***I have not defrauded offerings.***
6. ***I have not diminished obligations.***
7. ***I have not plundered the neteru.***
8. ***I have not spoken lies.***
9. ***I have not uttered evil words.***
10. ***I have not caused pain.***
11. ***I have not committed fornication.***
12. ***I have not caused shedding of tears.***
13. ***I have not dealt deceitfully.***

14. *I have not transgressed.*
15. *I have not acted guilefully.*
16. *I have not laid waste the ploughed land.*
17. *I have not been an eavesdropper.*
18. *I have not set my lips in motion (against any man).*
19. *I have not been angry and wrathful except for a just cause.*
20. *I have not defiled the wife of any man.*
21. *I have not been a man of anger.*
22. *I have not polluted myself.*
23. *I have not caused terror.*
24. *I have not burned with rage.*
25. *I have not stopped my ears against the words of Right and Truth. (Ma-at)*
26. *I have not worked grief.*
27. *I have not acted with insolence.*
28. *I have not stirred up strife.*
29. *I have not judged hastily.*
30. *I have not sought for distinctions.*
31. *I have not multiplied words exceedingly.*
32. *I have not done neither harm nor ill.*
33. *I have not cursed the King. (i.e. violation of laws)*
34. *I have not fouled the water.*
35. *I have not spoken scornfully.*
36. *I have never cursed the neteru.*
37. *I have not stolen.*
38. *I have not defrauded the offerings of the neteru.*
39. *I have not plundered the offerings of the blessed dead.*
40. *I have not filched the food of the infant.*
41. *I have not sinned against the neter of my native town.*
42. *I have not slaughtered with evil intent the cattle of the neter.*

M. M. NINAN

APPENDIX VI

THE SEVEN SPIRITS

"There shall come forth a Rod from the stem of Jesse, And a Branch shall grow out of his roots. The Spirit of the LORD shall rest upon Him, The Spirit of wisdom and understanding, The Spirit of counsel and might, The Spirit of knowledge and of the fear of the LORD". Isaiah 11:1-2

When Jesus became Man, the Son of Man, he was given the seven Spirits from God to make him the perfect man. Seven is God's number which represents perfection and it appears often.

These seven spirits that make man perfect are mentioned in Isaiah 11:1-2 as quoted above.

1. **THE SPIRIT OF THE LORD** is the (Ruah/ Pneuma) is central Spirit that connects man with God. This is the supernatural power source that creates God's Thoughts in our hearts

2. **THE SPIRIT OF WISDOM** (Chokmah / Sophia) #2451 *Chokmah (hokmah),* Wisdom, Word

3. **THE SPIRIT OF UNDERSTANDING** (Binah-Sunesis) is a perception, comprehension, and knowing the inner meaning of the raw data received. This spirit interprets the inner reality of the external experience.
#998 *Binah*: perfect understanding, derived from
#995 *biyn*, "to distinguish", "to separate mentally", "intelligence"

4. **THE SPIRIT OF COUNSEL** (Esa /Boulomai) is advocacy, direction, and instruction concerning life and daily living. This is what gives the judgment on which we base our choices
DETERMINE Lk.14.31. Act.5.33; 27.39. 2Co.1.17,17.
RESOLVE Jn.11.53.
CONSULT Jn.12.10.

5. **THE SPIRIT OF MIGHT** (Gibbor-Kratos) *gibbor* is a "man of might" or "hero,"

6. **THE SPIRIT OF KNOWLEDGE** (Daath-Oida) the "experiential" knowledge. Daath means Knowledge. "oida" means "to see, know, be

acquainted with";
#1877 *da'ath*: awareness or "secret knowledge"

7. THE SPIRIT OF THE FEAR OF THE LORD that gives us the basic force to live in righteousness.
This is the starting point of a righteous man. But he will grow beyond the fear of God into the love of God.
"The fear of the Lord is the beginning of wisdom" (*Ps* 11 :10; *Prov* 1: 7)
Heb 5:7 In the days of his flesh, Jesus offered up prayers and supplications, with loud cries and tears, to him who was able to save him from death, and he was heard for his godly fear.
Acts 10:34-35 Peter began to speak: "I now realize that it is true that God treats all men on the same basis. Whoever fears him and does what is right is acceptable to him, no matter what race he belongs to."
Jer 32:38-40 They shall become my people and I will become their God. I will give them one heart and one way of life so that they shall fear me at all times,.. I will fill their hearts with fear of me, and so they will not turn away from me.
Acts 9:31 Then the church... enjoyed a time of peace. It was strengthened; and encouraged by the Holy Spirit, it grew in numbers, living in the fear of the Lord.

Selected Works Vol I

Selected works of Prof. M.M.Ninan including: I AM - Symbols used by Jesus to explain himself; The Seven Churches of Revelation; The Kingdom Parables; A Study on Baptisml Perspectives on the Lord's Supper; When was Jesus Born? Genealogy of Jesus Theodicy, Anthropology and Demonology (God, Man and the Devil)

Selected Works Vol 2

This selection contains:

The History of Early Christianity in India; Hinduism is a Heresy of Thomas Christianity; History of the Malankara Churches; The Time Line of Christian History; Soteriology; Development of Mariolatory; Principles of Prosperity in the Kingdom of Heaven; Liturgy of St.James; Who is Melchizedek?; Christian Understanding of Trinity; God called the Sudanese before Israel!!

Selected Works Vol 3

Prophecy of Daniel,Quantum Theology,The Names of God,

Sola Scriptora- What does it mean?.

Cause Effect and the First Cause.A Study of Hebrews Chapter One

Land and Sea Reoutes of Early Christian Mission to India

Emergence of Hinduism from Christianity.

Life. Legacy and Theology of M.M.Thomas

Cultural Anthropology for Missions
Initially a once semester course in Sudan Theological College and a Missionary Orientation Course

Thy Kingdom Come
A Study of the central Judaeo-Christian concept of the Kingdom of God based on the Bible and the Mystical traditions of Judaism. It shows how the Kingdom principles of this world is an upside down version opposed to the Kingdom of God and redemption is accomplished through the cross alone. Based on the Bishop Easow Mar Timoteous Annual Lecture of 2008 by the author

Time Line Of Church History
This is a compilation of the major events in the church history showing the evolution of various churches and their theologies

Theodicy - Good God,Man, Evil, Devil And The Satan
DescriptionA study on Theodicy, Anthropology and Demonology explaining the concept of how evil can exist when God is defined as omnipotent, omniscient and Omni-benevolent.

Thinking Loud On Theodicy, Soteriology, Trinity And Hermeneutics
This is a study on the basic theological issues of Theodicy, Anthropology, Demonology , Soteriology, Trinity, and Hermeneutics. What is the nature of God? How do we explain the presence of evil and Satan? Are we predestined for Heaven and Hell? How many Gods have we? Three or One? How do we interpret the Bible?

Soteriology
A Study On God's Sovereignity, Human Freedom, Sin And Salvation

A Study on the problems and explanations on God's Sovereignity, Freedom of Will, Sin and Salvation

The Christian Understanding Of Trinity
An analysis of various understanding of Trinity within the Churches

The Seven Churches
This a study of the first three chapters of the book of Revelations to John.

Lord's Appointed Festivals
The Lord said to Moses, "Say to the people of Israel, the appointed feasts of the Lord which you shall proclaim as holy convocations, my appointed feasts, are these." Through these festivals which starts from Sabbath and end with Sabbath, Lord presented the world with a calendar of events which showed his Plan of Salavation of Mankind through history in a nut shell. This plan is explained by Prof. Ninan

Paul the Apostle is unique in that he was instrumental in embedding the Gospel of Jesus Christ into the Greco-Roman culture, the predominant culture of the period of Jesus. We have the complete documentation of Paul's ministry and his own writings form the basis of the doctrines and teachings of Christianity. His theology arises out of his scholarship in the Hebrew Priestly and Prophetic traditions both in its oral and written form. This book is an attempt to present Paul in these traditions which are handed down to us.

A detailed look at the Life and Mission of an Apostle of Jesus Christ who never walked with Jesus. Yet he was chosen to be the Architect and Builder of the Church and to define the doctrines of the Church of Jesus Christ. We look into the cultural matrix which created this great Apostle and his eventful missionary journey across the Greco-Roman empire and founded the religion which came to be known as Christianity.

A Study on Baptism
This is a detailed study on the various aspects of Christian baptism. Is Baptism necessary for salvation? What is the purpose and function of Baptism? What is the correct mode of baptism? What is the difference between Covenant Baptism and Believer's Baptism?

The Biblical Concept of Man
What is Man? What is his relation with God? Why is Man so important that God incarnated into the lowest realms of human existence? Professor Ninan develops two dimensional vector model of Man to explain the meaning of fall of man and reinterprets the Hebrew mystic ideas of Cosmos and Creation and the Theology of Theosis

I AM: Symbols Jesus Used to Explain Himself
During the end of his ministry, Jesus gave several statements which started with I AM in an attempt to explain who he really was. These symbols therefore give us an insight into the mystery of incarnation and process of redemption. These are explained in this book with the clarity of a scientist.

Kingdom Parables
In Mathew 13 Jesus tells a series of seven parables starting with the phrase "The Kingdom of God is like .....". Even though parables are not to be used as allegories, Jesus himself explained it as allegories and states that in years to come new meanings will be found in them. Here is an attempt to explain these seven parables as the development of Christianity through history. the point is that it fits.

Perspectives On The Lord's Table
DescriptionA study of the various historical and semiotic aspects of the Last Supper

Quantum Theology
The development of Quantum Theory has taken science to the limits of boundaries allowing for multidimensions and uncertainities. Prof. Ninan looks at some of the implication of the Quantum Theory in theology.

Semiotics of Sacraments

Understanding Sacraments

The Development Of Mariolatory
DescriptionA Study of the Development of the Roman Catholic Doctrine of Mariology,

Secrets Of The Prayer Shawl
Tallit the jewish prayer shall with its tassels were prescribed by the Lord as a memory device to remember the laws and statutes of the Judaic tradition. These meanings and symbolism are explained.

The Mysteries of the Tallit, the Tzitzit, and the Tekhlet
These are the Secrets of the Prayer Shawl given by Hashem. This is a study of the symbolism and meaning connected with the Biblical Prayer Shawl with its Tassels containing the mystic blue thread. The mesianic interpretation of the significance of the divine blue is studied. The rabinnic base is considered in some detail.

The Word Became Flesh
This is a collection of over a 100 paintings by Prof. M.M.Ninan. They include reproductions of Oil on Paper and of Digital Art. They are produced on the theme of Redemption and Recreation of Cosmos through the incarnation of Word in Flesh.

Angels, Demons and the Hosts of Heaven and Earth.
The basic Doctrines of Angelology, Demonology, Satanology, and all about the Hosts of Heaven and Earth – both good and bad. Based on the mystical understanding of Jewish tradition.

Rig Veda
Probably the oldest Hindu Scripture. Translation with collected help and commentaries by Prof. M.M.Ninan

The Vedas
This collection contains the following. The Yajur Veda, Sama Veda, Atharvan Veda. Brahma Samhita and Mantras

The Development of Hinduism

Traces the development of Hinduism from the ashes of Vedic religion under the varying influences of hero worship and local deities to the present form. The major forces were the coming of Christianity and of Persian Gnostics which molded it into the present form.

Sri Purusha Suktham
The Purusha Suktham occurs in the tenth mandala of Rig Veda. This is a Post-Christian work which portrays the influence of various religions of India at that time. This historical development is traced by Prof. Ninan and his commentary explains the influence of Christianity, Gnosticism and Brahmanism in this famous Suktham.

Isavasya Upanishad – the Immanence of Jesus

This is a unique interpretation of the Isavasya Upanishad which is based on historical and linguistic realities and overcomes difficulties otherwise encounterd by other eminent scholars like Sankaracharya.
Iswaran comes from the two sanskrit words Isa and paran, whch means Jesus is Lord. The word "Iswaran" came to mean God, only after the ministry of St.Thomas in India. This Upanishad is the doctrinal statement of the immanence and transcendence of Isa and his ability to provide release from death.

Riddles in Hinduism - B,R. Ambedkar
A detailed in depth study of the contradictions in the Puranas and the scriptures of Hinduism by Dr. B.R. Ambedkar, the father of Indian Constitution. His aim is to show the contraditions within the mythologies and the utter lack of coherence in the scriptures of Hinduism. The techniques of manipulative reinterpretation and circumlocution are used to confuse common people and to establish what is otherwise totally illogical. Dr. Ambedkar believed that this was with the ulterior motive of holding the masses under Brahminic domination.

Hinduism, What really happenned in India.
The religion known today as Hinduism is the Thomas Churches of Inner India established by St.Thomas which was high jacked by the Gnostics and Theosophists.

Prof. M. M. Ninan is a Professor of Theoretical Physics by training. He is specialized in Quantum Theory of Many Body Problem. He has taught Physics in the Universities around the world - Bombay (India, Royal Institute of Science), Ethiopia, Ghana, Jamaica, The Yemen Arab Republic, Sudan (Universities of Khartoum, Gezira and Juba), Bangalore (India) as well as in the United States of America. He was the President of the Hindustan Academy of Engineering and Applied Sciences of Bangalore University.

Prof. M.M.Ninan and his wife Mrs. Ponnamma Ninan –a sociologist, teacher –has extensively on the Bible in Yemen, Sudan, India and in the United States. He was the first Moderator of the International Christian Fellowship of the Yemen Arab Republic (the first Yemeni Christian Church established in Yemen since the massacre of Yemeni "Thomas Christians" by Islam in 6th c AD. He was one of the pioneers of the Sudan Pentecostal Churches and of the Sudan Theological College, where he taught theology for over five years during his tenure as Professor of Physics in the University of Juba in the South Sudan.

www.ingramcontent.com/pod-product-compliance
Ingram Content Group UK Ltd.
Pitfield, Milton Keynes, MK11 3LW, UK
UKHW041939190726
13854UKWH00004B/1686

9 780359 084975